WORKBOOK FOR
The ESL Writer's Handbook

Third Edition

JANINE CARLOCK

MAEVE EBERHARDT

JAIME HORST

University of Michigan Press   ANN ARBOR

Published in the United States of America by the
University of Michigan Press
Manufactured in the United States of America
Printed on acid-free paper

ISBN 978-0-472-03993-7 (print)
ISBN 978-0-472-22224-7 (e-book)

First published February 2025

Contents

Section 5. Grammar and Style (cont'd)

Section 6. Punctuation 97

If you are reading the ebook version of this book, please have some paper available to complete exercises.

Section One

The Writing Process

- Understanding Writing Assignments
- Generating Ideas

Understanding Writing Assignments
[Handbook, Section 1B]

Exercise 1.1: Key Words in Writing Prompts

For each group, write the letter of the definition in the right column next to the word it is defining in the left column.

Group A

1. ___ *summarize*
2. ___ *describe*
3. ___ *distinguish*
4. ___ *illustrate*
5. ___ *contrast*
6. ___ *critique*

a. give examples or an extended example
b. describe dissimilarities
c. provide the main points only, with no details
d. provide general statements and details that present a clear idea
e. evaluate the strong and weak points
f. describe the differences between two concepts

Group B

1. ___ *challenge*
2. ___ *assess*
3. ___ *prove*
4. ___ *define*
5. ___ *compare*
6. ___ *review*

a. describe similarities and differences
b. present and discuss the weak points of an argument or explanation
c. describe the general class to which a thing belongs and how it differs from all others in that class
d. explain why something is true
e. give a description of the issues involved
f. give a carefully thought-out judgment on something

Group C

1. ___ *outline*
2. ___ *enumerate*
3. ___ *address*
4. ___ *relate*
5. ___ *clarify*
6. ___ *trace*

a. explain the connections between two or more items
b. deal with, consider, discuss
c. provide a description that focuses only on main ideas, with no details
d. describe a series of events in sequence
e. give a descriptive list
f. explain in a way that makes the ideas easy to understand

Group D

1. ___ *explain*
2. ___ *interpret*
3. ___ *support*
4. ___ *defend*
5. ___ *list*

a. present facts to show that an explanation is true
b. provide information to make an issue clear
c. explain the meaning
d. give arguments to support a position or claim against criticism
e. provide a series of items

Group E

1. ___ *justify*
2. ___ *discuss*
3. ___ *state*
4. ___ *criticize*
5. ___ *process*

a. say what something is
b. something done in steps or stages
c. consider all aspects of an issue
d. give reasons for doing or saying something
e. evaluate the strong and weak points

Exercise 1.2: Identifying Key Words in Writing Assignments

Underline the key words in each writing assignment.

1. Discuss this proposition: All cultural and arts events and sites, such as libraries, concerts, museums, and festivals, should be made available to the public for free or at little cost. Defend your position with facts and examples.

2. Compare three of the sample proposals you have been given as representatives of the proposal genre. Analyze the language and organization and identify some key requirements for writing in the proposal genre.

3. Describe the process of photosynthesis. Provide diagrams to support your explanation.

4. Define the term "echo chamber." List the negative political and social impacts it can have.

5. Compare two of the great revolutions in world history. Evaluate the reasons behind and the results of each revolution.

6. Assess the benefits and drawbacks of attending a university in a foreign country. Enumerate at least three issues that a student should or should not consider when choosing to study abroad, and support your opinion with examples and personal anecdotes.

Generating Ideas
[Handbook, Section 1B]

Exercise 1.3: Brainstorming

Imagine that you are going to write an essay on one of these topics. Brainstorm ideas for one of these topics. Answers will vary.

1. Success

2. Technology in education

3. Sustainability in the field of X (your choice)

Exercise 1.4: Discussion (Pair or Group Brainstorming)

With a partner or a small group, discuss one of these topics. Write some new ideas generated by your discussion. Answers will vary.

1.   Having practical experience is better than knowing theory.

2.   National voluntary or military service should be required of all young people.

Exercise 1.5: Journalistic Questions

To help you generate more specific ideas for an essay, apply the journalistic questions (the Wh- *words:* Who? When? Where? Why? What? How?*) to one of these topics. Write responses to each question. Answers will vary.*

1. Internet addiction

2. English as a global language

3. Equity in healthcare

Exercise 1.6: Freewriting (Writing without Stopping)

Choose one of these topics. Freewrite for three minutes. Then underline some ideas from your freewriting that might be important to include in an essay on the chosen topic. Answers will vary.

1. Being a vegan/vegetarian vs. eating meat
2. Learning never ends.

Exercise 1.7: Listing

Select one of these topics. Then list some ideas related to that topic. Answers will vary.

1. Cybersecurity
2. Characteristics of a good leader

Exercise 1.8: Outlining

Choose one of these topics. Develop your ideas in an outline form by listing your main ideas and then adding more specific ideas under the main headings. Answers will vary.

1. healthy social media practices
2. working in the office vs. working remotely
3. traditional holidays and festivals
4. choosing a field of study
5. the importance of studying history
6. the value of alternative forms of energy (other than fossil fuels)

Exercise 1.9: Visual Mapping (Clustering)

Choose one of these topics. Create a visual map to generate ideas about it. Answers will vary.

1. use of AI
2. climate change
3. artificial intelligence (AI)
4. social media use

Exercise 1.10: Generating Ideas: Review

Choose one of the topics listed in the exercises above and generate ideas about it as if you are planning to write an essay. Use one or more of the idea-generating techniques that you did not already use for this topic to develop your ideas further: brainstorming, discussion, journalistic questions, freewriting, listing, outlining, or visual mapping. Answers will vary.

Section Two

Essay Structure

- Shaping a Paragraph
- Shaping an Essay

Shaping a Paragraph
[*Handbook*, Section 2A]

Exercise 2.1: Topic and Comment

Circle the topic and underline the perspective in each topic sentence.

1. My writing habits changed after taking the writing course.

2. There should not be mandatory curricula for young children.

3. Although both Shanghai and Hong Kong are cities in China, many cultural differences exist between them.

4. Parents should take responsibility for teaching their children how to behave, especially in a public environment.

5. Using a screen of any kind to keep a child under the age of three quiet can have harmful effects on a child's ability to focus later in life.

6. Activities that use fine motor skills, such as knitting and coloring, help increase manual dexterity.

7. Growing vegetables in a home garden is a healthy and cost-effective source of food.

8. To maintain a healthy lifestyle, you must monitor your diet carefully and exercise regularly.

Exercise 2.2: Finding a Topic Sentence in a Paragraph

Underline the topic sentence in the paragraph.

Recycling of paper products needs to be made a high priority by governments. This is because paper, one of the most commonly used materials in daily life, is made from trees, a resource that can easily be exhausted on the earth. Generally, after using paper, people just throw it away. It takes 30 to 50 years to grow a tree, but the time we take to use paper and throw it away can be just a few minutes. We cannot grow trees as fast as we exhaust them. As a result, too many of the world's trees will be destroyed unless we find good ways to deal with the used paper. Trees reduce the content of carbon dioxide in the air and improve the environment, providing valuable health benefits for humans. Therefore, we should recycle used paper products as much as we can in order to save trees for other uses and have a better environment as well.

Exercise 2.3: Writing Topic Sentences

Write a possible topic sentence for each paragraph. Answers may vary.

1. _____

   _____

   First of all, sports can make people healthy. When you do fitness exercises, you can strengthen your body. When you swim, you can improve your flexibility. In addition, sports can make people more cooperative. For instance, in a soccer team, 11 people play together. In order to play successfully and win games, the teammates must successfully cooperate.

2. _____

   _____

   Both debit and credit cards are more convenient than cash as a method of payment because money is always available through them. However, when you are using a credit card, you are borrowing money from the credit card company. You can repay it when you want, but you also have to pay the interest. With a debit card, on the other hand, you are using the money that is actually in your account. You are not allowed to overdraw, which means that you are not borrowing any money, and you do not need to pay any interest. Therefore, while debit cards have the benefits of credit cards, like convenience and safety, they also do not have the disadvantages of credit cards, namely, debt. In short, the use of credit cards should be discouraged, and debit cards should be encouraged in order to have more successful money management.

3. _____

   _____

   As part of my own community, I was influenced by certain social principles that contributed to shaping my life. For example, from my early childhood, I was taught by my parents to respect older people and help them, especially those who suffer from any kind of disability that could hinder certain aspects of their lives. This value led me to choose a major where I could help people: disability and communication disorders.

Shaping an Essay
[*Handbook*, Section 2B]

Exercise 2.4: Essay Introduction

Read this introductory paragraph of an essay written by a student. Then answer the questions below.

There has always been a strong argument about human nature. Some say we are born evil and others say we are born benevolent. It seems that this is an argument without a definite answer. However, I would say that human nature is gracious. I think such a view is very important in my life because it has encouraged me to do volunteer work and has led me to study education and pursue it as my career. Also, what is more important is that it has enabled me to live happily and optimistically.

1. What do you think is the main idea of the whole essay?

2. What are the main supporting ideas that you expect will be discussed in the body of the essay?

3. In what order do you think the supporting ideas will be discussed?

Exercise 2.5: Essay Conclusion

Read the concluding paragraph in an essay written by a student. Then answer the questions below.

To sum up, I cannot deny that giving college credits is a way to encourage students to be volunteers, and some might be inspired during their work. However, we should realize that there are great differences between the whole-hearted type and the half-hearted type discussed. The former enjoy their volunteer work, and it could have a good effect on them. On the other hand, the latter tend to be impatient and feel annoyed easily. The work could have a bad effect on them, and they may do the work badly. Thus, even if our society encourages students to work as volunteers for college credits, it will not cause them all to become more gracious and helpful in the long run because volunteer work is not something easy that needs only one's time. Instead, it is a job that needs one's heart.

1. Based on this concluding paragraph, what do you think is the main idea of the whole essay?

2. Based on this concluding paragraph, what are the main supporting ideas that you expect were discussed in the body of the essay?

3. In what order do you think the supporting ideas were discussed?

Exercise 2.6: Essay Introduction and Conclusion

1. *Underline the thesis statement of the essay in the introductory paragraph.*
2. *Underline the restatement of the thesis in the concluding paragraph.*
3. *Note the map (or foreshadowing) in the introductory paragraph, and list what you expect the main points of the essay will be.*

Introduction

A friend for me is a person whom I can trust and whom I can count on in different places and in different moments. Since about 1980, I can identify three distinct periods in my life in terms of my social environment and friendships. The first period started at the beginning of my elementary school and ended when I finished high school; the second started with my undergraduate studies and ended with my master's thesis; the last one began with my PhD studies and continues up to now. During all these periods of my life, I met different kinds of people and I made a lot of friends who were quite important to me.

Conclusion

Main points expected:

What I can conclude from this is that during all the time I have been a student, I have made many friends who have been a significant part of my life. I am convinced that nobody can live without friends. Certainly, if I hadn't made all these friends I would be a very different person today. In each stage of life, it is important to have people you can count on and who will help you on your journey through new challenges and experiences.

Exercise 2.7: Description

A. *Using descriptive language, write a brief paragraph (five to seven sentences) on one of these topics. Answers will vary.*

1. a teacher or role model that you remember from your childhood
2. a favorite song, musical composition, play, or movie
3. a beautiful or memorable place that you have visited
4. the process of making your favorite meal or dish
5. something you did that was challenging but that you succeeded in doing
6. a book that made a lasting impression on you

B. *Now review your paragraph, considering these elements of description:*

1. Circle any adjectives. Did you use enough adjectives and the most effective adjectives?
2. Comprehensive description: Did you provide description of various aspects of the person, thing, or situation to convey a clear sense of it to your reader?

Exercise 2.8: Simple Definition

Write a simple definition for each word. Answers will vary.

1. bus _____

   _____

2. mouse _____

   _____

3. cheese _____

   _____

4. calendar _____

   _____

5. sunscreen _____

   _____

6. headphones _____

   _____

7. elevator _____

   _____

8. umbrella _____

   _____

Exercise 2.9: Complex Definition

Write a complex definition (one brief paragraph) for each word. Answers will vary.

1. language

2. home

3. rice

4. friendship

5. online translators

Exercise 2.10: Examples

Find a sentence in the paragraph that needs an example or detail as support. Create a logical example and place it in the paragraph after that sentence.

Pacer Construction Company has demonstrated strong performance on past projects and has built a good reputation among its clients. Its strong performance is demonstrated by the fact that Pacer has finished all of its projects with good quality and on schedule, while often ending up under budget. Their excellent work is what has led to its good reputation. The company has received numerous awards demonstrating their high quality work. This recognition for its work directly reflects Pacer's work performance and the good reputation that it has built over four decades of construction experience.

Exercise 2.11: Paragraph Unity

This paragraph lacks unity because some sentences are not related to the topic. Make the paragraph more unified by crossing out the sentences or phrases that are not related to the main idea of the paragraph. Write the numbers of the deleted sentences below. [Sentences are numbered only for reference in this exercise.]

1 Diabetes can be divided into two categories. **2** One is Insulin Dependent Diabetes (IDDs, Type I diabetes) and the other is Non-Insulin Dependent Diabetes (NIDDs, Type II diabetes). **3** It is likely that everyone knows someone who has diabetes. **4** Both types of diabetes greatly increase a person's risk for a range of serious conditions such as blindness and kidney failure. **5** Thus it is important to have a good relationship with one's doctor. **6** Older people tend to have a wide range of health issues, including breathing difficulties, heart conditions, and circulatory problems. **7** Moreover, diabetics can have critical risk factors for heart disease, stroke, and leg amputations. **8** Although both types of diabetes are related with excess glucose concentration in blood, each has its own distinguished characteristics in causes, symptoms, and treatments. **9** Maintaining one's health can be quite expensive, especially when one must deal with serious health problems such as diabetes.

Sentences deleted to improve unity (write the sentence numbers):

Exercise 2.12: Creating Paragraph Coherence

The sentences of this paragraph, written by a student, have been moved out of their original order. Rearrange the order of sentences to create a coherent paragraph. Write the new coherent paragraph below. More than one order is possible. [Sentences are numbered only for reference in this exercise.]

1 Overall, the wine and champagne industries are very significant to the economic health of my hometown. **2** Once a year the people in the rural areas harvest those grapes and sell them to companies that make several kinds of wine, juice, and champagne. **3** Grapes are the main product that is cultivated in our region. **4** For people who like to know about wine and champagne there are several places where they can learn about the origin of the wine industry, see some of the local products, and taste some of the special wines and champagnes. **5** My hometown is a small, quiet city, and its economy is based on agriculture and tourism. **6** Additionally, tourism also makes its contribution to the regional economy.

Order of sentences to improve coherence (write the sentence numbers):

Exercise 2.13: Paragraph Coherence

These paragraphs lack coherence. Rewrite the paragraphs so that they are more coherent. Use transitions, repeated key words, synonyms, and reference words to improve coherence. Answers may vary.

1. My own experiences and my observations of others support the generalization that one must seek a deeper reason for the anger within oneself rather than looking to the outside. It is true that anger can be generated from relationships with others, but it is we ourselves who feel it. When we are frustrated by something, the degrees of anger vary according to our character, situation, place, and, scientifically, our genetic orientation. We have the experience of reacting differently to the same situation depending on our mood. We cannot rely on the external factors to change so that we can avoid anger because anger is an internal reaction to what is happening around us. Anger and the situations that cause anger are unavoidable, but we can train ourselves to deal with anger so that anger does not overcome us and affect other people in negative ways.

2. My family recently traveled to South America. We went to South America to have a vacation. We live in the United States. The United States is in the northern hemisphere. We visited Argentina. Argentina is in the southern hemisphere. It was July when we traveled. When we left home we were wearing t-shirts and sandals. When we got to Argentina we needed to put on coats and shoes with socks. In the southern hemisphere it is winter in July, and in the northern hemisphere it is summer in July. During our vacation it was sunny and it was not as cold as it is in winter where we live. We stayed for one month. It was funny that we needed such different clothing after just one plane ride.

Exercise 2.14: Using Transitions for Coherence in a Paragraph

Choose an appropriate transition word or phrase to fill each blank in the paragraph. Think about the logical connection that needs to be made between the ideas. Answers will vary.

The internet affects our lives in many ways today. **1** _____, we can communicate with each other by email easily, compared to sending messages by postal mail. **2** _____, we can chat with our friends, no matter where they are. **3** _____, we can buy whatever we want on the internet, and we do not need to go out to the shops. **4** _____, we can pay our bills such as electric fee and gas fee, and manage our accounts online. **5** _____, the internet has some disadvantages for people. There is too much information on the internet that is not very useful for us, and some information from the internet is not accurate at all.

6 _____, the internet reduces the interaction of people to some extent. **7** _____, your friend may just send an email to you instead of visiting you in person. That will decrease the opportunities for you to meet each other face to face.

8 _____, people can just chat at home on the internet rather than going out with their friends. **9** _____, while the internet may make our lives more convenient in many ways, the internet also decreases our social interaction and makes our lives more isolated.

Exercise 2.15: Using Transitions for Coherence in an Essay

The transitions have been deleted in this essay. Provide an appropriate transition for each blank space to create coherence. Answers will vary.

Employment and Taxes

Many developing countries face economic problems. Some people claim that the problems are too difficult to solve. There are, **1** _____, positive ways to improve the economic situation of countries and promote the lives of their poor people. These must include an increase in job opportunities and a decrease in the amount of taxes. Increasing employment and decreasing taxes will improve the economic situation of a country and reduce the rate of poverty.

2 _____, employment is the active engine that keeps a country going. It is the means by which people are able to care for themselves and their families. **3** _____, job opportunities maintain a certain economic security for people and enable them to improve their lives. This means that they can care for their families and be active, contributing citizens. **4** _____, jobs are a symbol of independence and self-sufficiency. A person who is self-sufficient does not need the help of governmental social programs like welfare or medical insurance for assistance in his or her life. **5** _____, this individual's self-sufficiency would save money for the government. **6** _____, unemployment is the negative condition that keeps an economy in an unfavorable and inactive state. Lack of employment is a serious problem for the individual in the sense that he or she will be and will feel dependent and lost.

7 _____, he or she may depend on the government to provide the basic needs for him or her. The government, **8** _____, loses resources and money in supporting such a person.

9 _____, another economic aspect that negatively affects a government is high taxes. Most people complain too much about the large amount of taxes they have to pay to the government. They claim that they cannot afford necessities because they find themselves left with little money. They cannot save money for later situations of need because the amount of their taxes is far out of proportion to their income. Taxes which are too great and which put a person in a tight situation badly affect the population and the economy. **10** _____, some economists assert that there should be low, fair, and balanced tax regulations that take into consideration people's personal financial situations and create opportunities for them to live a better life.

11 _____, despite economists' strong support of low taxes, it must be emphasized that they do not want taxes to be eliminated altogether. They realize governments must have revenues to use in social services and job creation. Before setting tax levels, governments should provide jobs to enhance people's economic situation. **12** _____, there should be a fair decision about the amount of taxes to be paid, taking into account the cost of living and the person's ability to pay a certain amount.

13 _____, high rates of unemployment and high taxes cause economic problems and lead governments into many financial crises. It is only by giving serious consideration to people's financial situations and providing them with jobs that an economy can be improved and stimulated.

Section Three

Patterns of Organization

- Narrative Essay
- Process Essay
- Comparison/Contrast Essay
- Cause-and-Effect Essay
- Argument Essay

Narrative Essay
[*Handbook*, Section 3A]

Exercise 3.1: Ordering a Narrative Paragraph

Put the sentences in narrative order by numbering them 1–13. (Hint: look for the topic sentence first!)

_____ a. Meanwhile, the campers, who were also excited and had been talking about how much fun the night was going to be, were devastated.

_____ b. I don't know what the others wished for, but I wished that I would again have as much fun at the next year's camp.

_____ c. When it rained heavily Wednesday night, the counselors were all upset because they wanted to have a last chance to all be together and have fun.

_____ d. Thursday morning we found out that that night was going to be one of the best nights for seeing meteor showers.

_____ e. One of my best memories took place when I was working at a children's summer camp last year.

_____ f. To help cheer the campers up, the counselors and campers had planned a big bonfire on Thursday and then a star-gazing session afterwards.

_____ g. After dinner, we and the campers all gathered in a big clearing by the lake and lit the bonfire we had prepared.

_____ h. It was the last weekend for many of the children at camp and everyone was feeling a bit sad.

_____ i. For hours, we all watched shooting stars together.

_____ j. Finding out about the meteor showers made the counselors deter-

mined that the bonfire should succeed.

_____ k. Then, as the bonfire died down, we all brought out our blankets and

lay down to look at the stars.

_____ l. The counselors were inspired to search all day for dry wood and set it

up for the bonfire in the evening.

_____ m. We all sang songs and roasted marshmallows, enjoying how the fire

lit up the night.

Exercise 3.2: Practice with *When* and *While*

Connect the sentences using when, while, *or* whenever. *If more than one can be used, write both answers on the line provided.*

1. _____ he was a junior in college, he met his future wife.

2. We were just leaving the baseball field _____ a tornado struck.

3. _____ I was watching TV, my brother came home from football practice.

4. _____ they learned that their daughter had been in an accident, they immediately rushed to the hospital.

5. _____ I was young, I used to spend a lot of time at my grandparents. I have fond memories of Sunday mornings spent reading the comics section with my grandfather _____ my grandmother baked homemade bread. To this day, _____ I smell freshly baked bread, I think of those happy times.

6. I had asked my neighbor many times not to play loud music in the afternoon _____ my baby was sleeping, but he would not stop. _____ I just couldn't take it anymore, I finally had to complain to the building manager.

7. At camp, since I didn't like to swim, I would help prepare lunch _____ the other campers were enjoying swimming in the lake.

8. Do you remember a day _____ you were so happy you wished that day could last forever?

Process Essay
[Handbook, Section 3B]

Exercise 3.3: Practice with Process Words and Phrases

Underline the process words or phrases in the paragraph. The first one has been done for you as an example.

How to Find a Doctor

Choosing a physician who will oversee your healthcare can be a difficult decision, but the process can be made less stressful by following a few simple steps. It is important to work through this process before you urgently need healthcare, so that you can make a wise and carefully thought-out decision. <u>An initial step</u> in this process is to ask friends for recommendations. Although your experience with a particular doctor may differ from another person's, these opinions can be very valuable in helping you to narrow your search to just a few doctors. Once you have a list of several doctors for whom you have received personal recommendations, you should call each office to ask a few questions: Is the practice accepting new patients? Can the doctor address your (or your family's) particular health concerns? You should also note whether the staff seem professional and friendly. Another very important step in this process is to find out whether your insurance company will cover visits to the physician that you select. You should check with both your insurance company and the doctor's office to verify this. If the answers to your initial questions are positive, a subsequent but optional step is to visit the office in person. Besides determining the convenience of the location, you can observe the atmosphere of the waiting room and examination rooms, and the personalities and mannerisms of the office staff and nurses. A visit also gives you the opportunity to interview the physician and ascertain his or her personality and approach to healthcare. To complete the process of selecting a doctor, you should inform both the doctor's office and your insurance company of your decision, so that there are no delays or complications when the time comes for you and your family to rely on your doctor's expertise.

Exercise 3.4: Connecting Ideas Using Process Words and Phrases

Connect and/or change the sentences to create a process paragraph. Not every sentence will need to be changed. Some sentences may need to be combined. Answers will vary.

How to Choose a Major

In choosing a major you should . . .

1. Talk with an advisor at your college or university.
2. Ask your friends if they know any good advisors at your college or university. Try to choose an advisor with interests similar to yours so you can be sure that he or she will have valuable information to share.
3. Tell the advisor about yourself.
4. Let the advisor know what you think your interests are.
5. He or she will give you advice about which departments might be the best for you.
6. Go to the department(s) that your advisor recommended and get more information.
7. Be sure to carefully consider the information you have collected.
8. Discuss the information and your options with friends and family.
9. Consider their advice and your own inclinations.
10. Make an informed decision.

Comparison/Contrast Essay
[*Handbook*, Section 3C]

Exercise 3.5: Connecting Ideas Using Comparison/Contrast Words and Phrases

Connect the pairs of phrases using comparison/contrast vocabulary. Try not to use the same connecting word(s) more than once. Write one comparison and one contrast sentence. Answers will vary.

Example

big cities / small towns

    a. ***Both** big cities **and** small towns must offer public education for their children.* [comparison]

    b. ***However,** in big cities, schools are usually overcrowded, **while** in small towns, classes are small.* [contrast]

1. *online shopping / shopping in a store*
    a.

    b.

2. *older people / younger people*
    a.

    b.

3. *fast food restaurant / sit-down restaurant*
    a.

    b.

4 *spending time looking at your friends' social media accounts / spending time with your friends in person*
    a.

    b.

5. *tropical climate / temperate climate*
    a.

    b.

Exercise 3.6: Using Comparison/Contrast Words to Create a Paragraph

Using comparison/contrast vocabulary, create an effective paragraph based on the framework of information given. First, use the chart to take notes. Answers will vary.

A. Studying at a large university	B. Studying at a small college
Class size:	Class size:
Facilities available:	Facilities available:
Relationship with teacher:	Relationship with teacher:
Variety of courses offered:	Variety of courses offered:
Number of clubs/extracurricular activities available:	Number of clubs/extracurricular activities available:
Dorm living:	Dorm living:
Other points:	Other points:

Cause-and-Effect Essay
[*Handbook*, Section 3D]

Exercise 3.7: Identifying Cause-and-Effect Words and Phrases

Underline the cause-and-effect words and phrases.

The Changing of the World with the Advent of the Internet

Imagine life before the internet. People waited in long lines to pay bills at banks. At the beginning of the semester, college offices were filled with students who wanted to register for their classes. When you couldn't find something in one store, you would have to drive to many others looking for it and perhaps just have to do without. Clearly, even though only a few decades have passed since the internet started to become commonly used, we can realize that the internet contributed to great changes in many parts of our lives.

First of all, the most important effect of the internet has been to increase accessibility of information. The internet allows people to get information easily, no matter the place or time. People do not need to go to the library and read several books to get information. That is because Google, the most popular web search engine, can show the web pages containing information people are searching within just a few seconds. Likewise, conventional encyclopedias in the library are not used so much any more because most people use Wikipedia, one of the biggest information providers on the internet. Thus, most students, researchers, and even common people would be very inconvenienced if the internet were no longer available. This demonstrates the important position the internet holds in our daily lives.

In addition, the internet has had an impact on facilitating interpersonal communication. For supporting examples one need look no further than email. Today, most students and workers turn on their computer in the morning and check email first. To send and receive email takes less than one minute. Many international students also use apps to talk with their family at any time or place. This definitely has resulted in positive outcomes for international students, who are far from home and may be feeling lonely due to culture shock. The fact that these students can easily communicate with their friends and family abroad leads to a sense of community and well-being that may help them through their period of culture shock.

Moreover, online shopping has become quite popular due to the ease with which you can order items from almost any store. Sites like Amazon have sprung up to meet customers' desire to receive what they want as quickly as possible and as cheaply as possible. Because customers do not need to drive to a store, they can save time as well as money. This is another way in which the internet has greatly affected our lives.

Finally, the most striking effect of the internet has been the advent of online services. Today, people use many kinds of online services. People often pay bills using online banking. Students tend to register for classes or hand in their homework online. Many governments provide online services including registration for the driver's test and photo ID to shorten citizens' waiting time at the office. Because it is so simple, using online services has become part of our daily lives as well, and the internet is the phenomenon that has made it possible.

The internet has greatly affected our lives. It helps us access information easily any place or time. We can communicate with those who live very far away using email and some websites allow us to shop at less cost and in less time. Furthermore, not only online shopping but also online services allow us to decrease the effort it takes to go to the store, bank, and government offices. Our lives have gradually changed due to the internet so that now we might even say it has become a necessity!

Exercise 3.8: Connecting Ideas Using Cause-and-Effect Words and Phrases

Use words or phrases to connect cause-and-effect ideas in the paragraph by filling the blanks. The first one has been done for you as an example. Answers may vary. [Sentences are numbered only for reference in this exercise.]

In the U.S. the divorce rate continues to rise every year. **1** <u>One reason for</u> this constant increase is the fact that divorces have become so common. Before the 1980s, divorced people were not viewed as the norm. The commonly accepted belief was that these people should have tried harder to work out their marital difficulties. Now, however, **2** _____ such a high percentage of married people get divorced, it may seem like a normal part of life. With more than 50% of marriages in the U.S. eventually ending in divorce, no one can take the attitude that divorced people are "strange." In addition, **3** _____ there is no longer a social taboo against getting a divorce, people do not feel compelled to "stick it out." **4** _____ a situation in which couples may go into a marriage thinking, "If it doesn't work out, I can always get a divorce." A typical **5** _____ of this kind of thinking is that when a difficult problem arises, rather than working hard to solve it or accepting that a compromise might be the only way to solve the problem, the couple uses divorce as a solution.

Argument Essay
[Handbook, Section 3E]

Exercise 3.9: Identifying Argument Words and Phrases

Underline the argument words and phrases used in the text. Remember that cause-and-effect expressions can also contribute to the development of an argument.

Early Computer Education: Its Negative Effects on the Intellectual Development of Children

Imagine a group of kindergarten students sitting in front of their screens in the computer room of an elementary school. They look into the dazzling images on their individually assigned computer screen while hardly talking to each other. No smile or liveliness can be found in this room, where these 6-year-old children start learning how to adapt themselves to the so-called age of information technology. Even though the computer is now an essential part of modern life, it doesn't seem logical to waste valuable childhood hours on a computer when children should be performing creative activities and discovering life for themselves. In fact, many people argue that computer education in early elementary years has several negative effects on the intellectual development of children: lowering their concentration on a task, preventing them from acquiring social skills, and exposing them to a hazardous online environment.

First of all, early computer education can lower children's concentration on a task. While young children learn on the computer, they use lots of software or computer games which contain attractive images. Even though they seem to pay attention to the work on the computer, actually they are just looking at the monitor, overwhelmed by the glittering pictures. This strong visual stimulation irritates children's minds and the children are apt to lose interest in things without such a dazzling display. To them, it may seem boring and dumb to read a storybook because it is not moving fast or shining with bright images. As a result, children can be easily distracted and cannot concentrate on the important tasks for their ages such as reading books, writing their opinions, or solving logical problems, which are definitely needed for their academic success and mental growth. We can deduce that this will lead to problems for the children later in life when these skills are necessary.

Another negative effect of early computer education is that children lose time and opportunity to socialize with peers. Because most children tend to work on the computer alone for a long time, they confine themselves in virtual space and are reluctant to interact with peers. Even though they need lots of social experiences in early childhood to grow into a well-rounded person, children can be easily involved in computer activity and may spend all of their free time doing something on the computer. Consequently, they are deprived of important opportunities to play and talk with their friends. It is reasonable to assume, then, that in this type of situation, where children grow up into adults without sufficient opportunity to interact with peers, they may have less of a capability to participate in our complex and interactive society.

Finally, children can be exposed to the hazardous online environment. For example, there is a great deal of inappropriate material on the internet like pornography, violence, and hatred. Those things exert a very bad influence on children. Because children are so sensitive and do not have much knowledge of life, they accept the dangerous influences as reality. In addition, they can encounter bullies or molesters via chatting or email. Due to the anonymity, a criminal can easily approach the innocent children and lure them into a very harmful situation. Therefore, children may experience physical danger as well.

In conclusion, early computer education may have a negative impact on children with respect to the development of concentration and social skills and to the possibility of harmful internet experiences. Therefore, it is better to teach children how to use a computer in their later elementary grades, taking into consideration their developmental stages. In doing this, we will be able to minimize the negative effects of children's computer education.

Exercise 3.10: Connecting Ideas Using Logical Argument

Create an argument by inserting sentences for B and C like in the example below. Answers will vary.

Example

A. Most college students have many things to do in addition to their schoolwork.
B. For example, many students have part-time jobs and participate in extracurricular activities such as sports and clubs. These activities may be time-consuming and can detract from the time students spend on studying.
C. Consequently, having tests helps students stay focused on their schoolwork.

Argument 1

A. The amount of violence in video games seems to be steadily increasing.

B.

C.

Argument 2

A. Antioxidants such as beta-carotene and lycopene are found in many fruits and vegetables.

B.

C.

Exercise 3.11: Making Generalizations

Write a generalization that can be made for each group of sentences. Answers may vary.

1. Heesung, Maria, and Abdullah are all students in Professor Huang's engineering class. Heesung has recently won an award for her research. Maria has a scholarship to study at the university for two years. Abdullah has been elected president of the Student Engineering Organization.

   Professor Huang _____

   _____

2. Akiko Yokohama has studied French for nine years. Her brother, Taro, works as a translator for a financial company in Germany. Their mother teaches English at a school in Tokyo.

   Members of the Yokohama family _____

   _____

3. In Hunter's Woods, 25 murders took place last year. There were also 53 cases of robbery and 10 drive-by shootings.

   The city of Hunter's Woods _____

   _____

4. Colleges are using online systems for grading. They are also using online systems for posting syllabi and offering orientation information online.

   Colleges _____

   _____

5. Parents use lullabies to help put their babies to sleep. Many hospitals use music therapy to help their patients feel better. Many people, after coming home from a long day at work, put some music on to help them relax.

   Music _____

   _____

Section Four

Research Paper

- Finding Sources
- Summarizing, Paraphrasing, and Using Quotations
- Outlining
- Writing Thesis Statements
- APA Style
- MLA Style
- Chicago Manual of Style
- IEEE Style

Finding Sources
[*Handbook*, Section 4B]

Exercise 4.1: Evaluating Sources

Imagine that you are writing a paper on the benefits of using technology in the classroom. Use an online search engine, Google Scholar, and/or your library's online research databases to find the source type listed. Provide brief notes for each of the criteria listed. Then answer whether you would use it in a research paper and explain your answer.

1. An online journal

Title of journal: _____

Title of article: _____

Author: _____

Source: _____

Relevance: _____

_____

Accuracy of information: _____

_____

Purpose: _____

_____

Currency: _____

Use this source? Yes / No / Maybe

Why or why not? _____

_____

2. A website

URL and title of website (or part of website): _____

_____

Author: _____

Source: _____

Relevance: _____

_____

Accuracy of information: _____

_____

Purpose: _____

Currency: _____

_____

Use this source? Yes / No / Maybe

Why or why not? _____

_____

3. An online news article

Title of newspaper: _____

Title of article: _____

Author: _____

Source: _____

Relevance: _____

Accuracy of information: _____

_____

Purpose: _____

_____

Currency: _____

Use this source? Yes / No / Maybe

Why or why not? _____

_____

Summarizing, Paraphrasing, and Using Quotations
[*Handbook*, Section 4D]

Exercise 4.2: Summarizing

Write a paraphrased summary of each passage from a student research paper in two or three sentences. (A paraphrased summary uses your own words or phrases, your own sentence structure, and your own order of information.) Try underlining important ideas, circling key words and phrases, and taking some brief notes.

Passage A

Smoking has become a big issue and a very common habit. Some people start with this habit because of stress, and others because they think it is "trendy." Despite the warnings given by doctors about negative side-effects of smoking, people continue to smoke and tend to not care a lot about it. Why is this serious problem underestimated by smokers? Is smoking really that dangerous? The truth is that tobacco contains many dangerous substances, including nicotine, which is a highly addictive drug that makes it difficult for smokers to quit. As we know nicotine is a dangerous and addictive substance, but cigarettes also have more than 4,000 chemical substances that are harmful for human health including benzene, arsenic, butane, DDT, toluene, and vinyl chloride (Healthy Living Now). Sixty-nine of these chemical substances are known carcinogens, meaning that they are known to cause cancer.

Furthermore, smoking for a long period (meaning 10 years or more) has progressive ill effects on the respiratory system. Lung disease is a common and serious illness in smokers who have smoked for at least a decade. The American Lung Association explains that some health problems develop very gradually, but after 10 years of tobacco use people's lungs are seriously damaged and smokers are in danger of death from emphysema. Smoking is responsible for 90% of all lung disease and 75% of chronic bronchitis. Clearly, smoking is a serious threat to people's health.

_____

_____

_____

_____

Passage B

Some may say that college is a place for nurturing and learning, and thus studying in college is not a big deal. However, many students spend a great deal of their time, mental focus, and physical energy on studying and feel a lot of pressure to get high grades.

Even those students who really love their majors and classes still need to put plenty of effort into their studies, which can bring on psychological stress and affect their physical health. College students work hard for many reasons—to have a high grade point average (GPA), to gain internships or research opportunities, and even to achieve successful jobs. To achieve all of this, students often trade their cheerfulness, sleep, social time, and hobbies to their GPAs. In a word, they are inevitably influenced by the expectation of high grades and trade their "life" to GPAs, placing their GPA over anything else.

Students who focus excessively on their grades, however, will find that many other parts of their lives are suffering. They may lose friends as they spend all of their free time with their books and computer rather than building relationships. They may fall ill or feel depressed if they do not allow themselves a healthy amount of time to eat, sleep, and exercise. And they might miss out on some of the exciting experiences that college offers—experiences that are unique to their years in college and that they will never be able to recreate after their college years are over. Students must realize that grades are not the most important thing in life—finding your life's passion and creating your own life values are a key part of your college education. For example, a student who values novelty, practicality, and creativity in life may choose engaging in a start-up technology company as a specific goal. High grades may not be the first priority of that student, but she will feel fulfilled and excited about her life's work. This is the best way to get the most out of college, rather than focusing only on having a perfect GPA.

_____

_____

_____

_____

Passage C

Fluctuations in global temperatures and climate patterns have been occurring for thousands of years, but global warming—a type of climate change that involves an increase in the Earth's average temperature—is becoming an increasingly serious threat for people nowadays. The Earth's population is increasing and so people are consuming more energy than in the past, causing increased levels of carbon dioxide in the atmosphere, which results in warmer temperatures on earth due to the "greenhouse effect." Some scientists warn of the possible threats to life on the planet as a result of global warming.

One possible effect of climate change could be the melting of ice in the Arctic and Antarctic regions. Some research has found that climate change has already had a negative impact on people's lives in the Arctic, in terms of the population of animals on which they rely for food. Melting polar ice will also lead to the rising of sea levels, which would lead to flooding that would destroy houses, farms, and the whole way of life for millions of people in coastal areas all around the world. There may also be a negative impact on people's health due to global warming. Some scientists predict that increases in global temperatures could cause faster reproduction of mosquitoes and a broader area where they can thrive, since they rely on warm temperatures to reproduce. Greater numbers of mosquitoes would likely result in higher rates of serious mosquito-borne diseases such as Zika virus, yellow fever, and malaria.

_____

_____

_____

_____

_____

_____

_____

Exercise 4.3: Recognizing Plagiarism

Each original sentence is shown together with the way it was used in a research paper. Decide whether or not the use is plagiarism. Explain your decision by writing the letter of the appropriate reason: A, B, C, D, or E.

Reasons:

A. Not plagiarism: Original words quoted with quotation marks and with citation.

B. Not plagiarism: Complete paraphrase with citation.

C. Plagiarism: Original words quoted but with no quotation marks.

D. Plagiarism: Some paraphrase but sentence structure is the same and some original words are quoted with no quotation marks.

E. Plagiarism: Quotation or paraphrase is correct but the citation is missing.

Source of Numbers 1–3: Unger, E. (2017, May 3). These salt flats are one of the most remarkable vistas on earth. *National Geographic*. Retrieved from www.nationalgeographic.com/travel/destinations/south-america/bolivia/how-to-see-salar-de-uyuni-salt-flats-bolivia/

1. **Original:** Stretching more than 4,050 square miles of the Altiplano, Bolivia's Salar de Uyuni is the world's largest salt flat, left behind by pre-historic lakes evaporated long ago.
   Use: The largest salt flat in the world, the Salar de Uyuni in Bolivia, was formed by now-evaporated prehistoric lakes and is over 4,050 square miles in area (Unger, 2017).

   _____

2. **Original:** Here, a thick crust of salt extends to the horizon, covered by quilted, polygonal patterns of salt rising from the ground.
   Use: A thick crust of salt goes all the way to the horizon, covered by polygonal patterns of salt that rise from the ground (Unger, 2017).

   _____

3. **Original:** This beautiful and otherworldly terrain serves as a lucrative extraction site for salt and lithium—the element responsible for power-ing laptops, smart phones, and electric cars.

Use: This "beautiful and otherworldly terrain" is also a source of both salt and lithium, which is used in a wide variety of electronics, from cell phones to electric cars (Unger, 2017).

———————

Source of Numbers 4–8: Panko, B. (2017, July 20). Humans have produced nine billion tons of plastic and counting. *Smithsonian.com*. Retrieved from www.smithsonianmag.com/smart-news/humans-are-burying-earth-under-billions-tons-plastic-180964125/

4. **Original:** New research shows that humans have produced just over 9 billion tons of plastic since 1950, with much of it still sitting around in our landfills and oceans.
   Use: Recent research shows that since 1950 people have produced over 9 billion tons of plastic, and much of this plastic remains in landfills and oceans (Panko, 2017).

———————

5. **Original:** Previous research has found that there may be more than 250,000 tons of plastic currently floating in Earth's oceans, much of it in the form of tiny chunks that can easily be carried by currents and consumed by sea creatures big and small.
   Use: The more than 250,000 tons of plastic dispersed throughout the oceans poses a great risk to a variety of sea creatures, both large and small, which may swallow the small pieces of plastic (Panko, 2017).

———————

6. **Original:** Some scientists have proposed using organisms to degrade the plastics, which left on its own rarely degrades in nature.
   Use: Since plastic does not naturally deteriorate on its own, scientists are examining ways to use organisms to break down the material (Panko, 2017).

———————

55

7. **Original:** The only permanent way to get rid of our plastic products is incineration, but only about 12 percent of plastic has ever met this fate. And researchers disagree about the safety of burning plastic, which has the potential to release a host of toxic chemicals into the environment.
Use: Although burning is a good way to dispose of plastic permanently, it is very rarely done and, when it is done, can release toxins into the air.

———————

8. **Original:** The most effective solution, however, may be changing our reliance on plastic.
Use: The best solution to the plastic problem may be to change our reliance on plastic.

———————

Source of Numbers 9–13: Kitchakarn, O. (2016). How students perceived social media as a learning tool in enhancing their language learning performance. *TOJET: The Turkish Online Journal of Educational Technology*, *15*, 53–60. Retrieved from https://eric.ed.gov/?id=EJ1117631

9. **Original:** Technology is currently being used to make teaching and learning more engaging and stimulating.
Use: Technology is currently being used to make teaching and learning more engaging and stimulating.

———————

10. **Original:** Apparently, Facebook is highly likely to prove advantageous to students should it be capitalized on as part of the learning process.
Use: Kitchakarn (2016) asserts that "Facebook is highly likely to prove advantageous to students should it be capitalized on as part of the learning process" (p. 53).

———————

11. **Original:** Even though this research revealed that students viewed Facebook favorably as an online learning tool, more studies should be conducted to find out whether and to what extent Facebook can help improve students' English competency in the long run.

Use: One study demonstrates that students have favorable opinions regarding Facebook as a tool in their language learning; however, in order to examine how useful Facebook can be in improving students' language skills over the long term, more research is needed.

————————

12. **Original:** In addition, choosing the right type of social media has a huge impact on participation.
Use: Participation is influenced strongly by the type of social media chosen (Kitchakarn, 2016, p. 60).

————————

13. **Original:** Facebook can be a platform of supplementary materials that teachers provide for learners to study outside class in order to gain knowledge.
Use: Facebook can serve as way to provide extra materials for students so that they can study outside class in order to gain knowledge (Kitchakarn, 2016).

————————

Source of Numbers 14–16: Beeler, C. (2017, July 21). A super-simple strategy may be key to fighting climate change. *PRI's The World*. Retrieved from www.pri.org/stories/2017-07-21/super-simple-strategy-may-be-key-fighting-climate-change

14. **Original:** In recent years, developed countries have committed billions of dollars to help developing countries prevent deforestation.
Use: According to Beeler (2017), "In recent years, developed countries have committed billions of dollars to help developing countries prevent deforestation."

————————

15. **Original:** A new study is the first to analyze a landowner payment program in a randomized trial—the gold standard of field research that is common in many areas of study but rare in conservation.

Use: A new study is the first to analyze a landowner payment program in a randomized trial—the gold standard of field research that is common in many areas of study but rare in conservation (Beeler, 2017).

———————

16. **Original:** If the program became permanent, Jayachandran estimated the cost of averting a metric ton of carbon would be $2.60, significantly less than the so-called social cost of carbon, which the Environmental Protection Agency in 2012 assessed at roughly $39.

    Use: Researchers estimate that long-term use of this program would incur a cost of $2.60 per metric ton of carbon averted, a significant difference from the Environmental Protection Agency's 2012 estimate of a social cost of $39 per metric ton of carbon (Beeler, 2017).

———————

Outlining
[Handbook, Section 4E]

Exercise 4.4: Ordering Outline Headings

The headings and subheadings of the outline below are listed in a jumbled order and with no indentation. Rearrange the list into an outline using the template to show the relative importance of ideas. Answers may vary.

Title: *The Benefits of Participating in a Study Group*

Get a support system

Several benefits to participating in a study group

Can practice new study skills in a group setting

Can contact someone in the group to get notes if you miss a class

Get new perspectives from discussion with other students

Helps you think more deeply about the topic you are studying

Can see how others study

Learn new study skills

Have someone to ask if you don't understand something in class

Understand the subject better

Main Idea: _____

1. _____

    a. _____

    b. _____

2. _____

    a. _____

    b. _____

3. _____

    a. _____

    b. _____

Writing Thesis Statements
[*Handbook, Section 4F*]

Exercise 4.5: Thesis Statements: Argument or Report?

Examine each sentence. If the sentence is the main focus of a **report paper**, *circle* **R**. *If it is the main focus of an* **argument paper**, *circle* **A**. *Also, if the sentence presents an argument, underline the key words that indicate it is an argument thesis statement.*

1. Over the past 15 years, companies have begun implementing many ways to make buildings more environmentally friendly.　　R　A

2. Although the United States has instituted several policies that require factories to reduce emissions, the penalties for not meeting the policy standards must be more consistently applied in order to achieve positive results.　　R　A

3. Those practicing modern medicine have recently begun exploring how more natural methods can be combined with technologically advanced treatments to achieve better outcomes.　　R　A

4. The European Union (EU) has experienced its share of financial difficulties; however, it should not be abandoned.　　R　A

5. The operating system of a PC computer is very different from that of an Apple computer.　　R　A

6. Publicly traded companies need to institute more effective oversight policies, or those in charge will continue to make decisions that benefit them personally rather than the stockholders, even if it means committing illegal acts.　　R　A

7. The completion of the railroad across the United States in the middle 1800s had far-reaching effects both socially and economically.　　R　A

8. Bioinformatics, the analysis of biological information using math and computer science, is a field that we must continue to invest in if we want to find better treatment for diseases like cancer or diabetes.　　R　A

9. Anthropologists define the word "tribe" in several different ways.　　R　A

10. Emma Watson is one of the best actresses of the twenty-first century.　　R　A

Exercise 4.6: APA References: Correcting Errors

Fix one error in each APA bibliographic entry.

1. Book
Loy, M. (2023). *Connecting communities in archaic Greece: exploring economic and political networks through data modelling.* Cambridge University Press.

2. Book
Salesh, B., and Jounell, G. (2017). *Giving up technology may just make your day* (2nd ed.). University of Chicago Press.

3. Edited book
Concueso, L. (Ed.). 2016. *Critical thinking: A collection of essays.* Stanford, CA: Stanford University Press.

4. Journal article
O'Toole, R.S. (2017). The bonds of kinship, the ties of freedom in colonial Peru. *Journal of family history, 42*(1), 3–21.

5. Chapter in an edited volume
Neruda, P. (2017). If you forget me. In M. Strand (Ed.), *100 great poems of the twentieth century* (pp. 21–22). New York, NY: W.W. Norton & Company.

6. Newspaper article
Maloney, J. (2024). U.S. pledges crackdown on illegal e-cigarettes. *The Wall Street Journal*, June 10. https://www.wsj.com/health/u-s-pledges-crackdown-on-illegal-e-cigarettes-2bf20794?mod=hp_lead_pos6

7. Book
Krawec, Patty. (2022). *Becoming kin: An indigenous call to unforgetting the past and reimagining our future.* Broadleaf Books.

8. Journal article
Buxton, R. & Draper, J. (2022). Refugees, membership, and state system legitimacy. *Ethics & Global Politics*, 15(4), 113–130. https://doi.org/10.1080/16544951.2022.2151286

MLA Style
[*Handbook, Section 4K*]

Exercise 4.7: MLA Works Cited: Correcting Errors

Fix the one error in each MLA bibliographic entry.

1. Book

deGrasse Tyson, Neil. *Cosmic Queries: StarTalk's Guide to Who We Are, How We Got Here, And Where We're Going*. National Geographic, 2021.

2. Book

Springfield, Janice, and Manchester, Simone. *A History of Immigrants in the US*. W.W. Norton and Company, 2012.

3. Chapter in an edited volume

Kendal, Dave, Emily Minor, and Monika Egerer. "People's Decisions Shape Urban Habitats." *Routledge Handbook of Urban Biodiversity*, Charles H. Nilon and Myla F.J. Aronson (Eds.), Routledge, 2024, pp. 111–26.

4. Journal article

Martinez-Austria, Polioptro F., and Erick R. Bandala. "Temperature and Heat-Related Mortality Trends in the Sonoran and Mojave Desert Region." *Atmosphere*, Vol. 8, No. 3, 2017, pp. 1–13.

5. Journal article

Maheux, Anne, et al. 2021. "Grateful: Longitudinal Associations Between Adolescents' Social Media Use and Gratitude During the COVID-19 Pandemic." *Journal of Research on Adolescence*, vol. 31, no. 3, pp. 734–47.

6. Newspaper article

Kevany, Sophie. "Wild horses return to Kazakhstan steppes after absence of two centuries." *The Guardian*, 10 June 2024. https://www.theguardian.com/environment/article/2024/jun/10/przewalskis-horses-only-wild-species-return-central-asian-steppes-kazakhstan.

7. Edited book

Gonzales, Laura, and Michelle Hall Kells, editors. *Latina Leadership: Language and Literacy Education across Communities.* Syracuse University Press. 2022.

8. Book

Pevar, Stephen L. *The Rights of Indians and Tribes.* Fifth edition, Oxford University Press, 2024.

Chicago Manual of Style
[*Handbook*, Section 4L]

Exercise 4.8: Chicago Works Cited: Correcting Errors

Fix the one error in each Chicago style bibliographic entry.

1. Book
Petcoff, Omonpee W., Janice C. Palaganas, and Marcel Danesi. Emoji in Higher Education: A Healthcare-Based Perspective. Cambridge: Cambridge University Press, 2024.

2. Book
Deaton, Angus. *The Great Escape: Health, Wealth, and the Origins of Inequality.* Princeton University Press, 2024.

3. Journal article
Sakeeny, Matt. "Textures of Black Sound and Affect: Life and Death in New Orleans." *American Anthropologist 126*, 2 (2024): 295–310.

4. Chapter in an edited volume
Silver, Blake R., and Graziella Pagliarulo McCarron. "Understanding College Students of Immigrant Origin." In *Supporting College Students of Immigrant Origin: New Insights from Research, Policy, and Practice*, edited by Blake R. Silver and Graziella Pagliarulo McCarron, pp. 3–16. Cambridge: Cambridge University Press, 2024.

Exercise 4.9: IEEE Works Cited: Correcting Errors

Fix the one error in each IEEE bibliographic entry.

1. Book
[1] N. Gredecki and P. Turner, Eds. *Forensic psychology.* New York, NY, USA: Routledge, 2022.

2. Journal article
[2] A. V. Kaplienko, B. A. Gabaraev, and Y. S. Cherepnin, "Potential role of nuclear power in a carbon-free world," *Nuclear Energy and Technology*, 10(2), pp. 89–96, 2024.

3. Journal article
[3] K. Olobatuyi, M.R.P. Parker, and O. Ariyo, "Cluster weighted model based on TSNE algorithm for high-dimensional data," *International journal of Data Science and Analytics*, vol. 17, no. 3, 2024.

4. Chapter in an edited volume
[4] Carroll, E.C. "Beyond the Watchdog: Using Law to Build Trust in the Press," in *Media and Society After Technological Disruption*, K. Langvardt and J. Hurwitz, Eds. Cambridge: Cambridge University Press, 2024, pp. 47–60

Section Five

Grammar and Style

- Word Form
- Articles
- Prepositions
- Word Choice in Formal Writing Style
- Reference Words
- Reducing Wordiness
- Subject–Verb Agreement
- Run-On Sentences and Sentence Fragments
- Comma Splice
- Adjective Clauses
- Parallel Structure
- Sentence Combining
- Sentence Variety

67

Word Form
[*Handbook*, Section 5A]

Exercise 5.1: Word Form Errors

Correct the word form error(s) in the sentences.

1. The lens acted as a prism, making the light looked like a rainbow.

2. Most of the mouse were used as control in the experiment.

3. The most common used material for computer keyboard is a type of polymer.

4. Historically, war are often fought because political entities decide they wants more land or resources.

5. The shipping of supply from the factory is usually done on Mondays and Wednesdays.

6. By law, families must use car seats for all child eight years old or younger.

7. After the invited speaker finished to talk, she took question from the audience.

8. It is important to be diplomat when dealing with a matter involving the development of a peace treaty among nations.

9. At the library you can find many different type of books.

10. Before write the paper, students should to make an outline.

Exercise 5.2: Word Forms

Fill in the blank with the correct word form. The base form of the needed word is provided.

1. After _____ [visit] his brother, Paul drove to Toronto.

2. Three _____ [woman] applied for the open position in the Sociology department.

3. In order to cook noodles, first you need _____ [boil] a pot of water.

4. The architect showed us several different _____ [design] for the entrance.

5. I was confused because the grocery store had been _____ [remodel] and the produce _____ [be] in a different location.

6. When we were standing next to it, the wind turbine was _____ [surprising] tall.

7. They did not see any other _____ [bicycle] while they were riding on the trail.

8. Physics _____ [be] one of her favorite _____ [subject] in school.

9. The little girl sang _____ [beautiful] in the _____ [crowd] auditorium.

10. You should _____ [research] carefully before _____ [buy] a car.

Articles
[*Handbook*, Section 5B]

Exercise 5.3: Articles

*In the paragraph, fill in the blanks with **a/an**, **the**, or **0** for zero article. Answers may vary in some contexts.*

My hobby is oil painting. I often go to **1** _____ museum to look at **2** _____ various paintings. Among **3** _____ artists on display at the museum, I prefer Maurice Utrillo, **4** _____ French painter who mainly drew Montmartre in Paris. Utrillo had three phases in his painting life: **5** _____ "montagny period," **6** _____ "colorist period," and **7** _____ "white period." I prefer **8** _____ paintings from the last phase. **9** _____ first paintings he did are only like imitations of **10** _____ Impressionists, and I find these canvases uninspiring. **11** _____ paintings from **12** _____ "colorist period" give us **13** _____ cheerful impression that is too bright for me. On the other hand, Utrillo's paintings from **14** _____ "white period" move me deeply. **15** _____ whitish colors with **16** _____ muted tones make me feel melancholy and contemplative. In addition, **17** _____ various tones of whites give me **18** _____ impressions of loneliness and isolation. I enjoy viewing **19** _____ Utrillo's paintings alone to feel those moods and emotions that only he gives us through his "white period," and when I paint **20** _____ pictures, I often imitate these tones because I wish to create **21** _____ similar melancholy feeling.

Exercise 5.4: Articles

Underline the nouns in each sentence. Circle the article used or put 0 above the noun if there is no article. Then explain why a/an, the, *or no article is used.*

1. Hallway walls need to be painted every two or three years.

   Explanation:

   _____

   _____

2. The letter that I just received is from an old friend.

   Explanation:

   _____

   _____

3. I bought coffee from the Starbucks in the student union.

   Explanation:

   _____

   _____

4. You can sometimes find examples of Early American furniture
   in museums.

   Explanation:

   _____

   _____

5. Universities often have libraries with special collections.

   Explanation:

   _____

   _____

Exercise 5.5: Looking at Nouns in Context to Determine Article Use

Underline the nouns in the paragraph from a student essay. For each noun, notice whether the, a/an, *or* zero article *is used with it. For each noun, give a reason for the type of article or zero article. [The sentences are numbered only for reference in this exercise.]*

Remember: The meaning of a noun may also be limited or made more definite by using demonstratives (e.g., *those*), possessives (e.g., *my*), and quantifiers (e.g., *some*). In such cases, articles are not used.

1 I remember one day when I was traveling to another city by train.

2 The journey was very long. **3** Sitting next to me there was a family who had annoying and unbearable children. **4** It was a long and frustrating day for me.

5 I had to bear the noise and misbehavior of the children. **6** I know that children make noise. **7** They go through a very energetic phase that is part of life.

8 That's their job. **9** The children were only being children, doing what children do. **10** However, there is a limit to everything. **11** Those children went far beyond the limit. **12** As a passenger, I am entitled to have a peaceful and quiet environment when traveling. **13** These parents should have worked harder to help their children to be quiet. **14** Before taking a long trip, parents should teach their children how to behave in a public place or when using public transportation. **15** In this way, neither the passengers nor the parents would have a hard time on their trip, and everybody would be relaxed, especially me!

Exercise 5.6: Articles

*In the paragraph, fill in the blanks with **a/an**, **the**, or **0** (for zero article). Be prepared to explain your answers. Answers may vary in some contexts.*

In **1** _____ United States, high levels of competition can affect **2** _____ social relationships among youth and adults, leading **3** _____ people to consider themselves as single individuals who should be ready to achieve their personal goals instead of being cooperative. Sometimes **4** _____ competitiveness prevents young people from just enjoying their activities; they forget that **5** _____ primary purpose of **6** _____ sports, music, and education is to enrich our lives and to teach us how to live in our society. It is **7** _____ problem because **8** _____ people are just focused on themselves. A major difference between **9** _____ values of the United States and my country, Venezuela, is that we don't believe as much as Americans in **10** _____ competition. We believe more in cooperation with each other. **11** _____ example is that in America to find **12** _____ job you need excellent skills and abilities to stand out from the rest of **13** _____ potential employees. However, in Venezuela you just need to know people—the more contacts and more friends you have, the better. That is **14** _____ culture of finding **15** _____ job in my country. Having **16** _____ friend or **17** _____ family member is what is going to increase the chances of getting **18** _____ employment. This shows how much we value **19** _____ relationships in my country, but it can be **20** _____ drawback because Venezuelans are more prepared to be friendly than to strive to be **21** _____ best.

Prepositions
[*Handbook*, Section 5C]

Exercise 5.7: Prepositions

In the paragraph, fill in the blanks with the correct preposition. The first two have been done for you as examples.

I did haircuts **1** <u>for</u> some friends recently, and I realized the process of hair-cutting is similar **2** <u>to</u> the writing process. When you start to cut hair for somebody, you need to figure **3** _____ the best style for this person, so you consult **4** _____ her or him, give some suggestions, and get some feedback. This is the same as generating ideas **5** _____ writing. Next you start cutting the hair **6** _____ the shape you designed. **7** _____ this stage, you don't work **8** _____ the details, but rather cut the hair **9** _____ each area such that you get a basic style. This phase compares **10** _____ drafting in writing. As you go on, you may find that the hairstyle you designed first is not good enough **11** _____ some ways. Therefore, you need to change it to fit the shape **12** _____ the person's face. Revising for writing is the same. Although this phase is similar for both hair-cutting and writing, there is a little difference **13** _____ them. In writing, you can delete some paragraphs and write new ones, but in hair-cutting you cannot put **14** _____ the hair that you have cut **15** _____. Last, when you are happy **16** _____ the shape and style of the haircut, you need to work **17** _____ some details, similar to the final editing stage in writing. You can smooth the edges **18** _____ the hair, or put some gel **19** _____ it, while in your essay you may want to check the spelling, punctuation, citations, or bibliography. After this, you can step back and admire your good work!

Exercise 5.8: Prepositions

In the paragraph, fill in the blanks with the correct preposition. Some blanks have more than one possible answer.

A Language of Wider Communication (LWC) is any language that allows communication **1** _____ speakers of different languages, either **2** _____ a single country or across national boundaries. In many countries, education is usually provided in the country's LWC, and the national LWC is generally used **3** _____ systems of government.

An LWC may be a language native to the region **4** _____ which it is used (such as Tok Pisin in Papua New Guinea), but this is not necessarily the case (as with English in many countries). Sometimes a country uses an LWC that is a local or regional language, not a major world language, which eases communication **5** _____ citizens of that country and enhances the sense of national identity. This is the case **6** _____ Uzbekistan, for example, where the official language (and LWC) is Uzbek, which is not widely spoken **7** _____ of that country. Other countries may select the language **8** _____ former colonizers as the national LWC, as did many of the former French colonies in Africa. This choice allows for easier communication **9** _____ national borders with other people who share the same LWC.

Exercise 5.9: Phrasal Verbs

In each sentence a phrasal verb (verb plus one or more prepositions) is under-lined. From the list of verbs, select one for each sentence to express a similar idea more formally. Use the correct form of the verb, and change any other grammar as necessary. The first one has been done for you as an example.

analyze	cancel	~~confuse~~	continue
discard	discover	finish	fluctuate
reduce	tolerate		

1. In his answer, Maurice <u>mixed up</u> two theories that should have been kept separate.

   In his answer, Maurice *confused* two theories that should have been kept separate.

2. Katherine can't <u>put up with</u> people who act in a superior manner.

3. We must carefully <u>break down</u> the components of this problem before we can find a solution.

4. When Anna <u>gets through with</u> the first project, she will immediately start the next one.

5. The dietician told me that I must <u>cut down on</u> my salt intake.

6. Octavia must <u>keep on</u> studying hard if she wants to pass the test.

7. Professor Benatar <u>found out</u> why the volcano was emitting lava.

8. Leo <u>threw away</u> the damaged equipment.

9. The data indicate that the temperatures <u>go up and down</u> a great deal.

10. Due to bad weather, we had to <u>call off</u> our field trip to the science center.

Exercise 5.10: Phrasal Verbs

In the paragraph, replace the phrasal verbs with single-word verbs. Answers may vary.

There are several factors to <u>think about</u> when choosing a major or career. First, when a hobby <u>turns into</u> a profession it places a financial burden on that job that might make people less passionate about it. Moreover, sometimes people <u>find out</u> that something they love to do as a hobby does not provide enough income for them to be financially stable. People who <u>look forward to</u> their hobby being their sole source of income may <u>end up</u> frustrated and discouraged when they realize this may be impossible. Even if it is not the primary thing that they love to do, someone can feel fulfilled by their job; in fact, they can likely both find satisfaction in their work and set aside time for their hobbies. People can surely <u>come across</u> opportunities to pursue their passion outside of work. Students need to carefully <u>think about</u> these points when <u>picking out</u> a major and a future career. Then they can <u>figure out</u> what is really the best path for them.

Word Choice in Formal Writing Style
[*Handbook, Section 5D*]

Exercise 5.11: Word Choice

This short essay includes a variety of informal and general words, some of which have been underlined. There may be additional words that you think are general and/or informal. Replace these words with more formal or specific words. Be prepared to discuss your answers. Some word changes may require changing the sentence structure or adding a longer noun phrase. Answers may vary.

When I left my country and moved away from my family, I needed to learn new <u>things</u>. For example, I was <u>awful</u> at cooking before I came here, but now I am a <u>good</u> cook. Furthermore, I eat <u>proper</u> food and pay more attention to what I eat because if I get sick, nobody will take care of me. Although I do not have <u>lots of</u> time to spend on eating and cooking, I still insist on eating regularly and at home.

Another effect of leaving my family is having to manage <u>everything</u> better and without help. For instance, I have more time than before, and I can decide how to spend it. I do not need to <u>get</u> permission to do anything. I have <u>made</u> a study schedule for myself and have been following it day by day. Moreover, it has already <u>taken</u> my parents <u>lots of</u> money to <u>let</u> me study here. Thus, I should manage my money <u>well</u> by not buying luxury <u>things</u>, comparing prices, and using coupons when I make purchases.

Finally, leaving my family and living by myself has been <u>good</u> for me because it made me <u>grow up</u> fast and <u>get</u> a sense of independence. It is very difficult for me to get used to this kind of life. Some <u>things</u> have changed and are different from before, such as my diet and my time and money management. However, I think I am <u>getting</u> an important and helpful learning experience for my whole life. Such experiences are <u>good</u> for all people.

Reference Words
[*Handbook*, Section 5E]

Exercise 5.12: Reference Words

Correct wrong or unclear references in each sentence, or insert synonyms in place of repetitive words or phrases. Answers may vary.

1. Professor Lee told Professor Dodd that her students were hard workers.

2. If the nations of the world all agreed to apply the same policies, they would be more successful.

3. Athletics at the Olympic level requires dedicated daily training. They actually spend years of their lives working towards this goal.

4. Several political campaigns were affected by unexpected global conflicts. The conflicts changed the way that voters viewed the candidates' positions.

5. Maria told me that there were two ways to interpret the experiment's results: one was that it was a well-conducted experiment and another was that its design was weak. I had not previously thought it was an issue.

6. The diplomats have refused to negotiate a ceasefire agreement, which is not acceptable.

7. The factory managers told the other employees that they would be getting an increase in their pay.

8. We emailed the office of the daily newspaper about the latest news, but it did not reply.

9. The typical romantic movie, it presents an unreal view of life.

10. Because of living there for a long time, Miguel said that I should be able to speak Spanish fluently.

Reducing Wordiness
[Handbook, Section 5F]

Exercise 5.13: Reducing Wordiness in Sentences

Revise the sentences to reduce wordiness. Answers may vary.

1. Tyrone's argument is not very persuasive because it is a weak argument that provides little evidence to show that it is valid.

2. After reading her report, we decided that the hiring policy regarding new workers should not be applied in our consideration of the hiring of anyone new.

3. If economists were to base their recommendations only on the data they receive from corporations, their recommendations would not be based on enough information to give good advice.

4. It is the opinion of Ms. MacDonald that we should not support any politicians who promise that everything will become perfect in the future if we vote for them.

5. From my viewpoint, study skills are very important skills that we can acquire that will help us when we are studying in school or college to advance our education.

Exercise 5.14: Reducing Wordiness in a Paragraph

Revise the paragraph to reduce wordiness. Answers may vary.

These days there are many people exhibiting different types of behavior. Usually people's attitudes in a society and their behavior toward each other and society depend on the education and training they received from their parents when they were young, and that affects their future and their whole lives later on. Based on my own experience and people's habits in a society, it can be shown that parents influence their children's future. During my childhood, my parents taught me good values, the kind of attitudes that should be adopted socially and in every way, according to each situation of my life. In order to give me some proofs and examples, they also used to put into practice these values whenever it was necessary for them, and I grew up with those kinds of attitudes. They taught me honesty, integrity, and courtesy toward all.

Subject–Verb Agreement
[Handbook, Section 5H]

Exercise 5.15: Subject–Verb Agreement

If there is an error in the sentence, write I (for incorrect) in the blank, and correct the error. If there is no error, write C (for correct) in the blank.

___ 1. Even though the answer are correct, the way in which you got the

answer is not clear.

___ 2. Each of the 12 questions have only one correct answer.

___ 3. They decided to meet on Thursday to finish writing their programs,

which are due on Friday.

___ 4. In order to resolve these problems, we need to first look at what is

causing them.

___ 5. Neither my teacher nor my advisor know the answer.

___ 6. Many of the characters in the novel *The Lord of the Rings* are based on

beings from Celtic mythology.

___ 7. Both of the societies that we are studying in our textbook right now

seems to share a common ideological foundation.

___ 8. It has been shown that the majority of the population in each of those

countries does not vote in the annual election.

___ 9. It is difficult to determine whether the parent or the child were

to blame.

___ 10. The news these days are full of stories of violence.

Exercise 5.16: Subject–Verb Agreement

Write the suggested verb in the blank, making sure that it agrees with the subject.

Mastering a skill **1** _____ [require] many hours of practice and hard work. Some people **2** _____ [suggest] that 10,000 hours of practice **3** _____ [be] necessary before truly becoming a master in a particular skill. But is 10,000 hours a useful number, or is mastery more a matter of natural talent and dedication? I believe that it's neither skill nor hard work. Very few people **4** _____ [reach] elite levels of athletic, musical, intellectual, or artistic achievement. I do not believe that everyone who **5** _____ [practice] a skill for more than 10,000 hours will become renowned for their skill. Someone who **6** _____ [work] hard for many years will certainly be highly skilled in their field. But will they be a master? It is difficult to judge that. My brother, along with several of his friends, **7** _____ [have] been practicing judo for more than ten years. They are all quite skilled and each of them **8** _____ [have] competed at the national level. There **9** _____ [be] no doubt that they have worked quite hard and have achieved a high level of skill in judo. Are they masters in their sport? Have they reached the 10,000-hour mark? A better question may be: Are they pursuing their passion and reaching their full potential while maintaining physical and emotional health? This, rather than a mythical 10,000 hours of practice, **10** _____ [be] the best way to measure success.

Run-On Sentences and Sentence Fragments
[*Handbook*, Section 51]

| Exercise 5.17: Run-On Sentences and Fragments

Correct any run-on or fragment errors. Answers may vary.

King Louis 14th demanded that artists paint him as a god or mythological person. And add more dignity to his portrait. The king was thus depicted wearing clothes of the emperors of ancient Rome and Greece. To send a message that he was the legitimate successor of the ancient empires. In these paintings, there were also goddesses and legendary heroes around the king. To impress people with his honorable character.

Moreover, the height of the king in paintings was always bigger than his real height all of the images were made to strengthen the authority of the king and government.

The famous palace of Versailles was also designed to represent the authority and the power of the king in the clearest way. In this palace, many bureaucrats and noble families lived around the king, who was the center of the court the paintings or statues of him, as well as his symbols, were placed everywhere in the palace. People were surrounded by works of art. That were well planned to give a particular impression of the king. Therefore, it was difficult for citizens to be indifferent to the existence of the king at this palace.

Exercise 5.18: Fragments

Revise the sentences in the paragraph to correct the three sentence fragment errors. Answers may vary.

In King Louis 14th's era, arts and new technologies were the most important ways of advertising. He and his court encouraged many kinds of arts and technology. To represent the power of the king. In the field of art, he established an organization of painters and patronized many artists. Including famous sculptors and architects. The Académie Française was established at this time. Since he wanted scholars to be studying the French language and to be cultivating it. In the field of science, we can say that the establishment of the national astronomical observatory was one of this king's main achievements.

Comma Splice
[Handbook, Section 5J]

Exercise 5.19: Comma Splices

Correct the comma splice errors in the paragraph. Answers may vary.

Everyone needs smiles! You need a smile, for example, when you feel lonely or blue. When you are happy, it takes no effort to smile because it is already there. However, when you feel down, it is good to smile, how? It is easy. Lift the edges of your lips. You do not need a big smile, just a little lift makes your mind lighter and warmer. I have to say that I do not know why this works, however, I have heard about a relationship between the physical and mental systems, they are interactive, when you are happy, a smile appears on your face. When you make a smiling face, you can make yourself feel happy. After I heard about this, I tried it, it worked!

Adjective Clauses
[*Handbook*, Section 5K]

Exercise 5.20: Comma Use in Adjective Clauses

Correct the errors in adjective clauses in the paragraph. Answers may vary.

The liver is the most important organ that is affected by alcohol. The liver which is the largest organ in the body removes or detoxifies poisons, germs, and bacteria from the blood, makes protein, and produces immune agents. Although direct damage from alcohol in the liver cells has not been reported, alcohol and its metabolites injure the liver by blocking its normal metabolism of proteins, fats, and carbohydrates. As a consequence, consuming alcohol on a regular basis causes fatty liver, alcoholic hepatitis, and alcoholic liver cirrhosis which all prevent the normal functioning of the body. In addition, bleeding, that cannot be stopped easily, develops when the protein-making function of the liver is destroyed. Gallstones, itching, and jaundice which is the yellowing of the skin and eyes also result because of deteriorating bile metabolism. If the liver is not able to detoxify poisons from the blood, these toxins accumulate in the blood and finally in the brain. People, who have these problems, are likely to suffer from personality changes, mental symptoms, coma, and even death.

Parallel Structure
[*Handbook*, Section 5L]

Exercise 5.21: Parallel Structure

Find and correct errors in parallelism in the paragraph. Answers may vary.

Governments frequently divert what science produces into war-related uses. The original reason for scientists inventing things is usually to improve technology and helping people live better. For example, the purpose of inventing the airplane was to shorten travel time, and dynamite was invented for people to remove mountains and they could build houses there more easily. However, governments changed the purpose of those technologies. The airplane has been changed into a military equipment transporter or carrying bombs, and they made dynamite into a killing tool in these bombs. It is true that people spend a lot of money on researching new technology for a better life; however, a lot more money is spent for development of the new technology into new weapons.

Sentence Combining
[*Handbook*, Section 5M]

Exercise 5.22: Combining Sentences

Combine the pairs or groups of simple sentences. Try to change the meanings as little as possible. Answers may vary.

1. Memory is a vital quality of human thought. Without memory we would not be able to function in our daily activity.

2. Memory failures do happen frequently. This causes many problems, such as forgetting important information that we studied for an exam.

3. When studying for an exam, you can use different techniques to improve how much you remember the important points. You can highlight the points in your textbook with a marker pen. You can write a summary of the important points on file cards. You can recite the important points out loud to yourself.

4. I make up possible exam questions based on my class notes. It's a study method I learned from my aunt. She was a professor of psychology. This method has always been the most effective one for me.

5. Study your class notes before a test. Put the notes aside. Then say the main points out loud, as if you are telling someone what they are. It will help you remember them.

6. I learned a valuable study method from my friend. My friend Andre seems to remember his class notes very well. It helped me a lot.

7. Andre advised me not to leave my studying until just before a test. He said that I should have shorter study sessions of the same material every day. He had found this approach to be much more effective than trying to remember everything in one long study session.

8. Memory is affected by repetition. Highlight the important points in your textbook. Read them again and again over a period of several days.

9. Some students use mnemonics to help them remember facts. A mnemonic is a memory aid. A mnemonic can be a made-up word, a verse, or other verbal or visual device.

10. I found it hard to remember the colors of the rainbow. Then I learned a simple mnemonic that sounds like a person's name. The mnemonic is "Roy G. Biv." It uses the first letter of each color: red, orange, yellow, green, blue, indigo, violet.

Exercise 5.23: Using Specific Structures to Revise Sentences

Rewrite the sentences using the suggested structure. Combine sentences when necessary. Answers may vary.

1. I was very unwilling to take the course in trigonometry. I took the course. [**adverb**]

2. During the 1980s Tim Berners-Lee developed the foundation of what we now call the Web with his work on information retrieval from distributed systems. [**passive**]

3. We missed our flight due to Stanley's failure to arrive on time. [**divided sentence**]

4. Janae had studied hard for the final examination in her Biology class. She was sure that she would do very well on it. [**dependent clause**]

5. Paulina was encouraged by her good results on the final History exam. She thought that she might take a more advanced course in the next semester. [**participial phrase**]

6. Alexander Fleming discovered penicillin when he observed that mold would not grow around a bacteria culture that he had unintentionally left uncovered. **[passive]**

7. Alfonso traveled to Ecuador, where his family was still living. He was happy to go there. **[adverb]**

8. I did not say "basketball." I said Enrico is very skilled at tennis. **[divided sentence]**

9. I wished that I had studied harder for the spelling test. I arrived at school in a state of anxiety. **[participial phrase]**

10. It was not easy to develop a new research program to better understand how the sun transmits radiation. Professor Bigelow and her graduate students were successful in their work and published an article about it. **[dependent clause]**

Sentence Variety
[*Handbook*, Section 5N]

Exercise 5.24: Creating More Variety in Sentence Structure

Rewrite the paragraph so that there is more variety in the sentence structure. Answers may vary.

The use of fossil fuels has increased greatly. Coal, natural gas, and oil are fossil fuels. Fossil fuels have negative effects on the environment. Using more ethanol would be better than relying too much on fossil fuels. Ethanol has advantages that are clear. Ethanol's big advantage is that it can be made from many common crops. Sugar cane, corn, and wheat are examples of possible sources of ethanol. Growing more of these crops can help farmers increase their income. However, humans and livestock also need these crops for food. A choice has to be made sometimes between growing crops for food and growing crops for fuel. It's a difficult choice. Reducing the supply of food crops may cause an increase in food prices. Many of the world's people are hungry and need these crops as food. However, with cheaper fuel, farmers can grow crops more efficiently. They use fuel-powered equipment for planting and reaping crops. This can increase their production of crops.

Section Six

Punctuation

- Period [.]
- Question Mark [?]
- Exclamation Point [!]
- Comma [,]
- Semicolon [;]
- Colon [:]
- Double Quotation Marks [" "]
- Single Quotation Marks [' ']
- Apostrophe [']

Period [.]
[Handbook, Section 6A]

Exercise 6.1: Period at End of Sentence: Correcting Run-On Sentences

Each sentence has a punctuation error that has resulted in a run-on sentence. Correct the error by inserting a period in the appropriate position. Correct capitalization as necessary.

1. Machines can be helpful if you understand them some people don't like any machines.
2. When the sun is shining, I go swimming when it rains, I go swimming too because I love swimming.
3. Monarch butterflies have a very distinctive look they are a beautiful orange color with black and white markings.
4. I would very much like to travel to foreign countries as soon as possible which ones I will go to will not be certain until I determine the costs of air travel.
5. The raw material of statistics is data or numbers the data are the result of counting or measurement that assigns numbers to objects.
6. Biostatistics focuses only on biological and medical science areas there are many biostatistics applications in clinical data.
7. Descriptive statistics is organizing and summarizing data to determine what information the data contain to organize and summarize data, we can use methods such as order array or measuring the central tendency by mean, median, and mode for population or grouped data.
8. Diabetes can be divided into two categories one type is Insulin Dependent Diabetes and the other is Non-Insulin Dependent Diabetes.
9. It is important to drink enough water to avoid dehydration many people do not drink enough water doctors recommend 8 glasses a day.
10. There are many problems in the field of global education basically they arise from the fact that so many children do not attend primary school, so more advanced education is not possible.

Exercise 6.2: Period at End of Sentence: Correcting Errors

In each paragraph, the wrong punctuation has been inserted where the periods should be. Make the necessary corrections.

1. Clara looked out to sea, to her left were some ships? Far beyond the ships, she saw some whales and dolphins, she saw only cliffs and crashing waves to her right, she decided then that she would try to find a ship that would accept her as a passenger for the long journey across the ocean? She was determined to cross the Pacific and begin her search—

2. Omar didn't know where he had left his keys? He looked all over the house for them, he couldn't seem to find them in any of the usual places. He had to go to work he would be late! He realized that maybe they were in an unusual place? He looked under the cushions of the living room sofa and he looked under the refrigerator, he spent more than an hour looking for them, finally he found them in a plant on the windowsill …

Question Mark [?]
[*Handbook*, Section 6B]

Exercise 6.3: Question Mark and Period

Some of the sentences in the paragraph are questions, and some are not. Place periods or question marks in the appropriate places. Capitalize as necessary. Remember that a question mark is not placed after indirect (reported) questions.

The detective sat in his office thinking about the strange events at the time of the crime These were his thoughts: Who was the second witness why had she vanished so quickly there were many people who wanted to know he knew that Anne wanted to know Sally had asked questions about it Andrew had also made inquiries James, however, had asked only two questions he had asked when the crime occurred he had also asked why it had been committed that was very strange why had James not asked about the second witness Did he perhaps know where she was it would probably be a good idea to question James about his movements after the crime

Exclamation Point [!]
[*Handbook*, Section 6C]

Exercise 6.4: Exclamation Point for Strong Feeling

Decide which of the following sentences or phrases express strong feeling and place exclamation points after them. In other cases, use a period or question mark.

1. Oh, wow
2. Did you find the new location easily
3. The painting was rather unusual, with a turtle shown in a strange mixture of green, blue, pink, and various shades of red
4. How strange
5. Who is that man carrying the book
6. I can't believe I forgot
7. Are you able to come to the meeting
8. What an amazing opportunity

Exercise 6.5: Exclamation Points, Periods, or Question Marks in a Conversation

Place exclamation points, periods, or question marks in the appropriate places in the dialogue.

Customer: How much is this pair of shoes

Clerk: Ninety-nine dollars

Customer: That's so expensive

Clerk: Not really, considering what they are made of

Customer: What are they made of

Clerk: A special, rare material originally designed for astronauts' boots for use in space

Customer: How amazing perhaps I'll buy a pair

Clerk: Great What size shoes do you wear

Customer: Size 12

Clerk: Oh no That size is out of stock

Customer: Oh well I guess I won't be buying these shoes today

Comma [,]
[Handbook, Section 6D]

Exercise 6.6: Comma after Introductory or Transitional Words and Phrases

Place commas, if needed, after the introductory words and phrases in the sentences.

1. It is customary to place a comma after introductory or transitional words and phrases.
2. Remembering all the serious obstacles faced the previous year Kamila refused to try again.
3. Having gone over the material carefully in study group Dominique felt ready for the test.
4. As a means of repairing torn cloth nothing could be better than this special machine.
5. Being a lazy student from my earliest schooldays I naturally found it hard to pass examinations.
6. Natalie had become fluent and had made many new friends during her semester abroad.
7. After speaking to his bank manager the wheat farmer was able to get a loan to enable him to continue farming for another year.
8. At the restaurant Ivan and Olga met many journalists whom they had not seen for 15 years.
9. The letters that were addressed to me were finally delivered to the right address.
10. Except for the writing class my studies at the Language Institute are very easy.
11. Once they understand English comma usage the students will find all the other marks of punctuation relatively easy.
12. Moreover it was absolutely impossible for the ambassador to visit the Prime Minister.

Exercise 6.7: Comma after Introductory Clauses

Place commas, if needed, after the introductory clauses in the sentences.

1. When winter comes Kenji hopes to go skiing.
2. He will buy a bag of oranges if he goes to the supermarket.
3. After Oscar's cousin arrives in Tasmania they will travel together to the north of the island.
4. Very many students agree that the university offers excellent courses.
5. Unless they can travel to an English-speaking country students must learn the language in their own countries.
6. Students who want to learn English travel to English-speaking countries if they can.
7. Because certain unusual events have occurred the detectives are investigating the case.
8. Many people do not smoke because it would affect their health.
9. If my phone is broken I will need to replace it right away.
10. Since it rained all day we were not able to go to the park.

Exercise 6.8: Comma before Coordinating Conjunctions Linking Independent Clauses

Place commas, if needed, before the coordinating conjunctions in the sentences. When both clauses are very short (about five words or less), the commas can be left out to emphasize a strong connection between the clauses.

1. There has been an increase in the popularity of volleyball and many more spectators are attending the games.
2. Some of the tennis players were doing special exercises to improve their game but others were just relaxing in the clubhouse.
3. My cousins did not like golf nor did they like cricket.
4. Vincent will travel to Uruguay to start a new branch of his business or he will stay in his country for two more years and then go to Uruguay.
5. My chemistry teacher keeps very busy since he also does a lot of research.
6. They left the house on time but they were late to the theater because of an accident.
7. Kumiko gave me advice and I succeeded.
8. Coffee was the only drink available at the small cafeteria so we drank many cups of strong coffee.
9. The research teams in the computer industry always try to find out what the competition is working on and they then try to bring out similar or better products.

Exercise 6.9: Comma with Lists of Words, Phrases, or Clauses

If the sentences include a list of three or more words, phrases, or clauses, separate the items from each other by placing a comma after each item in the list.

1. Books papers bottles cans pens and pencils were lying scattered on the floor of the room.
2. Sonam decided to study economic theory business administration personnel management and computer programming.
3. Jennifer's sister could not decide whether to study art French or linguistics.
4. Hassan refused to go to the store because it was raining very hard because he felt tired and because there was enough food in the house.
5. If a politician smiles at you promises you something wonderful claims to have done many good things or criticizes his opponents, you can guess that there must be an election soon.
6. Financial advice loans and credit cards were all offered by the new bank.
7. The travel advertisement promised an ideal holiday in South America, with visits to Brazil Paraguay Argentina and Chile.
8. The journalist said that all countries need to diversify their energy sources find more fossil fuels and conserve fuel supplies in order to ensure that energy resources are adequate.
9. The complaints to the mayor mentioned problems with parking facilities traffic flow public transportation unsafe pedestrian crossings and special paths for bicycles.
10. Swimming walking jogging and dance are all good forms of exercise for busy students.

Exercise 6.10: Comma with Coordinate Adjectives

Separate coordinate adjectives from each other by placing a comma between them. Do not place a comma between the last adjective and the noun. Do not separate cumulative adjectives. (Adjectives that can be joined by and are coordinate; adjectives that cannot be joined by and are cumulative and are not separated by commas.)

1. Senator Pulinski is a tough outspoken critic of the President's foreign policy.
2. A big fluffy gray cat is always coming into our yard.
3. It was a difficult bumpy long twisting road that led to the farmhouse on the side of the mountain.
4. Yiwen said that her history class was always interesting very informative and quite stimulating.
5. Due to a severe system-wide problem with spam and viruses, our company installed a complicated computer protection program on all our machines.
6. Our walk in the woods turned out to be cold wet and tiresome instead of the pleasant relaxing stroll that we had expected.
7. The best exhibit in the art gallery was a ten-foot-wide concrete and metal statue of a horse and rider.
8. The Queen's chefs prepared a delicious mildly spicy special dish for her 15 dinner guests.
9. Even though she was tired, the loud buzzing noise kept her awake.
10. The Himalayas, where Mount Everest is located, are a huge awe-inspiring mountain range in Asia.

Exercise 6.11: Comma with Quotations

Place commas before and after the direct quotations (the words actually spoken). Leave out the comma when a quotation begins or ends a sentence and when the quotation ends with a question mark or exclamation point.

1. Yoo-Jin wrote "These two advertisements can be compared in several aspects."
2. "The women's salaries are higher than the average salary of men in that business" asserted Nina.
3. "Excuse me," the customer asked "where can I find the reference section?"
4. "But that was my idea!" Sachiko exclaimed.
5. "This design will appeal to young, fashionable people. We must use it in our next product" said the artist to the manager.
6. "I prefer" said Hannah, pointing at the book "to stay at home alone to read this. It's so interesting! It's about English grammar."
7. "The style and purpose of this musical composition are fascinating" said Jessie.
8. "Online purchases were more than half of the sales in the first quarter, signifying a major new direction for the company" according to a report released by Frew and Macmillan Corporation.
9. A professor of business studies wrote "In electronic transactions, transparency of price, design, availability, and supplier produces more choices and better pricing."
10. "Industrial development near the city is the key to our progress" announced the mayor.

Exercise 6.12: Comma with Abbreviations

Place commas, as needed, in the sentences.

1. This course for first-year students helps with many things e.g. study skills time management etc.
2. The important issue in this election is tax credits for individual citizens i.e. indirectly returning some funds to them.
3. During the test you must remove all bags, books, papers etc. from the desk.
4. Abbreviations should be limited to situations where they help the reader i.e. when comprehension would be increased by using them.
5. Take some extra food, clothing etc. on this trip because it may take longer than planned.
6. Several new books have been published recently on this topic e.g. *The Brain's Way of Healing*.

Exercise 6.13: Comma with Contrasting or Interrupting Elements or Those Needing Separation for Clarity

Place a comma, if needed, before and after contrasting or interrupting elements or those needing separation for clarity. Omit the first comma if the interrupting element begins the sentence. Omit the second comma if the interrupting element ends the sentence.

1. Amelia's husband by contrast is a strict vegetarian.
2. This computer though high quality is not the type they need.
3. Therefore the square of the hypotenuse is equal to the sum of the squares of the other two sides.
4. Would you like to sing now Ms. Johnson?
5. Our shoes are you know the best available even if they are the most expensive.
6. Students who want to attend college must be very diligent.
7. Sounding quite excited she spoke about her trip to New Zealand.
8. I accepted the suggestion of painting the walls red and orange because the room needed brightening.
9. Will you please be as quiet as possible during the recording?
10. Secondly place the apples in a dish with the other fruit.
11. My flute which I got for my 12th birthday is one of my most prized possessions.
12. Our reading teacher bought a fine vehicle from the second-hand car dealer on Forbes Avenue.
13. We arrived in this great city in September of 1977.
14. Angela despite her injured foot won the long jump.
15. This book not the one that is on the table is his.
16. I think that given no serious or unexpected obstacles we will complete our research project before the middle of March.

Semicolon [;]
[Handbook, Section 6E]

Exercise 6.14: Semicolon with Independent Clauses

Use semicolons to separate independent clauses, coordinate clauses, or items in a list. Pay close attention to the other punctuation in the sentences for clues as to where to place the semicolons.

1. All flights in and out of the airport have been canceled the storm is predicted to hit early this afternoon.
2. Do not go back to the beginning if you make a mistake just keep going until you finish the job.
3. There was a variety of objects lying on the floor: old books, most of them with torn covers sheets of paper, thrown down by the clerks empty containers, which had obviously been used for paint and many empty shoeboxes.
4. After the party we returned to school, driving along the old highway, a dangerous road, luckily for us, we made it back safely.
5. In order to use the machine you should first remove the dust cover then press the green button, which starts the motor going then turn the speed control, at the top left, to the desired speed and, finally, adjust the heat control to the desired temperature.
6. The traveling circus transported many things, including large tents animals, safely secured in cages musical instruments of all types and costumes that were specially designed for each performer.
7. The film, which was very interesting, helped us to understand the special uses of magnetism, electricity, and heat and the presentation, as usual at such conferences, was followed by a general discussion.

Exercise 6.15: Semicolon

Necessary semicolons have been left out of the sentences. Insert them in the appropriate places.

1. When Stefan's order arrived, I opened the box and was surprised to find an enormous blue hiking backpack with reflective stripes a high-tech water filtration device that included a rechargeable battery a pair of lightweight, collapsible hiking poles and a waterproof map of the North Country Trail.

2. A lot of money is spent on preserving our nation's water supply, which involves taking care of rivers, lakes, dams, and reservoirs but it remains a difficult task.

3. Everything went wrong yesterday: the children, who were late for school, started fighting my car, bought just a month earlier, would not start my best friend, recently recovered from a serious illness, called to say he was feeling sick again and my boss, a pleasant, kind man, told me that I might lose my job.

4. The photocopier seemed to be failing: the paper kept getting jammed there were large dark streaks in the middle of all the copies and the machine gave an error message when it was turned on.

5. The first problem is that, in order to pay college fees, students must get loans, grants, or scholarships and the second problem is that they must study hard to pass the difficult exams.

Colon [:]
[Handbook, Section 6F]

Exercise 6.16: Colon

Place colons in the appropriate places in the sentences.

1. They purchased many things after winning the lottery two new cars, a vacation home and a boat.

2. She read two long novels over her winter break *Anna Karenina* and *The Tale of Genji*.

3. Our class meets on Tuesdays at 9 45, not 8 45.

4. In the introduction to his famous book, *The Origin of the Species*, Charles Darwin begins

   When on board H.M.S. "Beagle," as a naturalist, I was much struck with certain facts in the distribution of the organic beings inhabiting South America, and in the geological relations of the present to the past inhabitants of that continent. These facts, as will be seen in the latter chapters of this volume, seemed to throw some light on the origin of the species—that mystery of mysteries, as it has been called by one of our greatest philosophers.

5. The young boy had the following in his pockets string, used chewing gum, pebbles, a catapult, some pennies, twigs, a broken pencil, and a few marbles.

6. The Japanese poet Basho once said "Do not seek to follow in the footsteps of the wise; seek what they sought."

7. Professor Nicholas began to write the recommendation letter for her best student, which began,
   To the Admissions Committee
   I am writing in support of Clara Morgan's application to your PhD program in Civil Engineering.

8. For this recipe, use a ratio of 3 1 (three to one)—three parts water and one part rice.

9. The odds against my horse winning are 5 2 (five to two).

10. As Ismael cleaned his room, he found the following items under the bed a dirty sock, two of his favorite comic books, and the homework assignment he could not find the night before.

11. To his surprise, Guiseppe found three English proverbs that referred to Rome "All roads lead to Rome," "Rome was not built in a day," and "When in Rome, do as the Romans do."

12. Leilani's daily work schedule is as follows check for mail, reply to urgent letters, attend meetings, have a business lunch, work with the planning department, and finally, attend to mail orders.

Double Quotation Marks [" "]
[*Handbook, Section 61*]

Exercise 6.17: Double Quotation Marks

Insert double quotation marks where needed in the following sentences. Remember to capitalize the first word of the quotation when needed.

1. My father reminded me, don't take Moore Street because it's under construction and the bridge is closed to traffic.
2. The contract states, we reserve the right to void any service fee at our discretion.
3. Salma quietly suggested, maybe you should wait until you're feeling calmer to write that email. It's usually not a good idea to send a message while you're angry.
4. The phrase burning the candle at both ends means that someone is trying to do too many things and will probably run out of time and energy.
5. Tameka announced that everyone would be receiving a $500 bonus due to the success of the program.
6. Please tell me more about your prior work experience, the manager requested.
7. I don't know why the bus was so late, Fernando complained. There was hardly any traffic so late at night.

Single Quotation Marks [' ']
[*Handbook*, Section 6J]

Exercise 6.18: Using Single and Double Quotation Marks

Insert single and/or double quotation marks where needed in the following sentences. Not all sentences will contain both types of quotation marks. Remember to capitalize the first word of the quotation when needed.

1. I went to the little shop downtown to buy sandals for my vacation, Sachi explained. I thought the clerk was very rude when she said, that's ridiculous. We don't carry sandals in the winter. I'll never go back there again.

2. Johann read aloud the opening sentences of the story: Elisa looked out the window. Sophia, she whispered, I think someone's out there.

3. I don't know why you're asking me these questions, the agent stated. My lawyer told me not to discuss anything until she arrives.

4. You didn't say, come to my house at 7 pm, Jerrell argued. You said, let's meet at 7 pm.

5. Lucia boldly stood up and proclaimed, the student committee has discussed this matter and is in agreement that that board decision is wrong.

6. The latest update says, the authorities will provide more information when it becomes available, but there's nothing else written, grumbled Mariam.

Apostrophe [']
[Handbook, Section 6M]

Exercise 6.19: Apostrophe

Insert the apostrophes where they are missing in each sentence. Some sentences contain more than one error.

1. The childrens shoes were lined up neatly by the door.
2. The farmers equipment was damaged in the flood, and he didnt know how hed finish the harvest.
3. Aria wasnt sure if Evas phone had been repaired.
4. The football players uniforms were yellow with black stripes.
5. "Were going to the beach on Saturday," my mother announced. "I think well all benefit from getting out of the city."
6. Thomas didnt realize that his passport had expired until after hed bought a plane ticket.
7. All of the countrys leaders will gather at the Prime Ministers residence next week, where theyll discuss the many issues that the citizens are facing.

Answer Key

Section 1. The Writing Process Answer Key

Exercise 1.1: Key Words in Writing Prompts (page 2)

Group A
1. c *summarize*
2. d *describe*
3. f *distinguish*
4. a *illustrate*
5. b *contrast*
6. e *critique*

a. give examples or an extended example
b. describe dissimilarities
c. provide the main points only, with no details
d. provide general statements and details that present a clear idea
e. evaluate the strong and weak points
f. describe the differences between two concepts

Group B
1. b *challenge*
2. f *assess*
3. d *prove*
4. c *define*
5. a *compare*
6. e *review*

a. describe similarities and differences
b. present and discuss the weak points of an argument or explanation
c. describe the general class to which a thing belongs and how it differs from all others in that class
d. explain why something is true
e. give a description of the issues involved
f. give a carefully thought-out judgment on something

Group C
1. c *outline*
2. d *enumerate*
3. b *address*
4. a *relate*
5. f *clarify*
6. e *trace*

a. explain the connections between two or more items
b. deal with, consider, discuss
c. provide a description that focuses only on main ideas, with no details
d. describe a series of events in sequence
e. give a descriptive list
f. explain in a way that makes the ideas easy to understand

Group D
1. b *explain*
2. c *interpret*
3. a *support*
4. d *defend*
5. e *list*

a. present facts to show that an explanation is true
b. provide information to make an issue clear
c. explain the meaning
d. give arguments to support a position or claim against criticism
e. provide a series of items

Group E
1. d *justify*
2. c *discuss*
3. a *state*
4. e *criticize*
5. b *process*

a. say what something is
b. something done in steps or stages
c. consider all aspects of an issue
d. give reasons for doing or saying something
e. evaluate the strong and weak points

Exercise 1.2: Identifying Key Words in Writing Assignments (page 3)

1. <u>Discuss</u> this proposition: All cultural and arts events and sites, such as libraries, concerts, museums, and festivals, should be made available to the public for free or at little cost. <u>Defend</u> your position with facts and examples.

2. <u>Compare</u> three of the sample proposals you have been given as representatives of the proposal genre. <u>Analyze</u> the language and organization and identify some key requirements for writing in the proposal genre.

3. <u>Describe</u> the process of photosynthesis. Provide diagrams to <u>support</u> your explanation.

4. <u>Define</u> the term "echo chamber." <u>List</u> the negative political and social impacts it can have.

5. <u>Compare</u> two of the great revolutions in world history. <u>Evaluate</u> the reasons behind and the results of each revolution.

6. <u>Assess</u> the benefits and drawbacks of attending a university in a foreign country. <u>Enumerate</u> at least three issues that a student should or should not consider when choosing to study abroad, and <u>support</u> your opinion with examples and personal anecdotes.

Exercise 1.3: Brainstorming (page 4)

Answers will vary.

Exercise 1.4: Discussion (Pair or Group Brainstorming) (page 5)

Answers will vary.

Exercise 1.5: Journalistic Questions (page 6)

Answers will vary.

Exercise 1.6: Freewriting (Writing without Stopping) (page 7)

Answers will vary.

Exercise 1.7: Listing (page 8)

Answers will vary.

Exercise 1.8: Outlining (page 9)

Answers will vary.

Exercise 1.9: Visual Mapping (Clustering) (page 10)

Answers will vary.

1. Use of AI

2. Climate Change

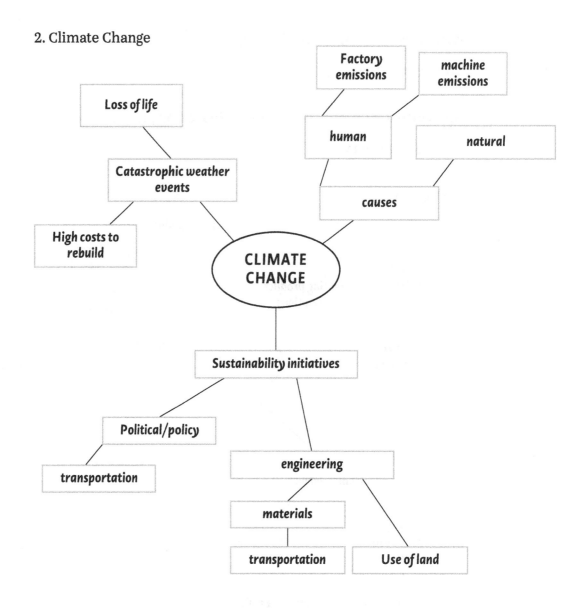

Exercise 1.10: Generating Ideas: Review (page 11)

Answers will vary.

Section 2. Essay Structure

Exercise 2.1: Topic and Comment (page 14)

1. (My writing habits) changed after taking the writing course.

2. There should not be (mandatory curricula for young children.)

3. (Although both Shanghai and Hong Kong are cities in China,) many cultural differences exist between them.

4. Parents should take responsibility for (teaching their children how to behave,) (especially in a public environment.)

5. (Using a screen of any kind to keep a child under the age of three quiet) can have harmful effects on a child's ability to focus later in life.

6. (Activities that use fine motor skills, such as knitting and coloring,) help increase manual dexterity.

7. (Growing vegetables in a home garden) is a healthy and cost-effective source of food.

8. (To maintain a healthy lifestyle,) you must monitor your diet carefully and exercise regularly.

Exercise 2.2: Finding a Topic Sentence in a Paragraph (page 15)

Recycling of paper products needs to be made a high priority by governments. This is because paper, one of the most commonly used materials in daily life, is made from trees, a resource that can easily be exhausted on the earth. Generally, after using paper, people just throw it away. It takes 30 to 50 years to grow a tree, but the time we take to use paper and throw it away can be just a few minutes. We cannot grow trees as fast as we exhaust them. As a result, too many of the world's trees will be destroyed unless we find good ways to deal with the used paper. Trees reduce the content of carbon dioxide in the air and improve the environment, providing valuable health benefits for humans. Therefore, we should recycle used paper products as much as we can in order to save trees for other uses and have a better environment as well.

Exercise 2.3: Writing Topic Sentences (page 16)

Answers will vary.

1. <u>Participating in sports has many benefits.</u> First of all, sports can make people healthy. When you do fitness exercises, you can strengthen your body. When you swim, you can improve your flexibility. In addition, sports can make people more cooperative. For instance, in a soccer team, 11 people play together. In order to play successfully and win games, the teammates must successfully cooperate.

2. <u>Using debit cards as a method of payment is better than using a credit card.</u> Both debit and credit cards are more convenient than cash as a method of payment because money is always available through them. However, when you are using a credit card, you are borrowing money from the credit card company. You can repay it when you want, but you also have to pay the interest. With a debit card, on the other hand, you are using the money that is actually in your account. You are not allowed to overdraw, which means that you are not borrowing any money, and you do not need to pay any interest. Therefore, while debit cards have the benefits of credit cards, like convenience and safety, they also do not have the disadvantages of credit cards, namely, debt. In short, the use of credit cards should be discouraged and debit cards should be encouraged in order to have more successful money management.

3. <u>Every community has its own cultural values that influence the lives and thoughts of the individuals living in that community.</u> As part of my own community, I was influenced by certain social principles that contributed to shaping my life. For example, from my early childhood, I was taught by my parents to respect older people and help them, especially those who suffer from any kind of disability that could hinder certain aspects of their lives. This value led me to choose a major where I could help people: disability and communication disorders.

Exercise 2.4: Essay Introduction (page 18)

1. Main idea of the essay: <u>Human nature is gracious</u>
2. Main supporting ideas: <u>connecting "gracious" to volunteering, studying education, and living happily and optimistically</u>
3. Order of supporting ideas: <u>the same order as in the thesis statement at the end of the introduction (see #2 above)</u>

Exercise 2.5: Essay Conclusion (page 19)

1. Main idea of the whole essay: <u>2 types of volunteers—whole-hearted and half-hearted</u>
2. Main supporting ideas: <u>whole-hearted type enjoy it and it has a positive impact; half-hearted type has a negative impact and they don't do a good job</u>
3. Order of supporting ideas: whole-hearted then half-hearted volunteering

Exercise 2.6: Essay Introduction and Conclusion (page 20)

1. <u>During all these periods of my life, I met different kinds of people and I made a lot of friends who were quite important to me.</u>
2. What I can conclude from this is that <u>during all the time I have been a student, I have made many friends who have been a significant part of my life.</u>
3. Main points expected:
   <u>Stories from each period of education named in the introduction in that order: beginning of my elementary school to end of high school; undergraduate studies to master's thesis; beginning of PhD studies up to now.</u>

Exercise 2.7: Description (page 21)

Answers will vary.

Exercise 2.8: Simple Definition (page 22)

Answers will vary.

bus <u>A bus is a type of vehicle that travels roads and is used to transport many people from one place to another, including the general public, school children, or church groups.</u>

mouse <u>A mouse is a small, usually gray or brown, herbivorous rodent that has a long tail, makes a squeaking sound, and lives under the ground.</u>

cheese <u>Cheese is a food made from the solid material that is left behind after curdling milk.</u>

calendar <u>A calendar is a place where people can write in their daily or monthly schedule to help them remember what appointments they have each day.</u>

sunscreen <u>Sunscreen is a lotion or spray that you put on your skin before going into the sun to protect it from ultra-violet rays and sunburn.</u>

headphones <u>Headphones are a type of equipment that has a covering for each ear connected by a band that goes over your head, which people listen to music or other information through.</u>

elevator <u>An elevator is a machine found in building with more than one floor that can move several people up and down in a building at one time so they don't have to use the stairs.</u>

umbrella <u>An umbrella is a common accessory that people carry with them to shield their head and body from rain.</u>

Exercise 2.9: Complex Definition (page 23)

Answers will vary.

Exercise 2.10: Examples (page 24)

Answers will vary.

Pacer Construction Company has demonstrated strong performance on past projects and has built a good reputation among its clients. Its strong performance is demonstrated by the fact that Pacer has finished all of its projects with good quality and on schedule, while often ending up under budget. Their excellent work is what has led to its good reputation. The company has received numerous awards demonstrating their high quality work. <u>Some examples of awards that they have won are the Stricko Award for Excellence in Construction and the Justus Award for Top Customer Service the past five years.</u> This recognition for its work directly reflects Pacer's work performance and the good reputation that it has built over four decades of construction experience.

Exercise 2.11: Paragraph Unity (page 25)

Sentences deleted to improve unity: 3, 5, 6, 9

Exercise 2.12: Creating Paragraph Coherence (page 26)

Order of sentences to improve coherence (the sentence numbers): 5, 3, 2, 1, 6, 4

Exercise 2.13: Paragraph Coherence (page 27)

Answers will vary.

Exercise 2.14: Using Transitions for Coherence in a Paragraph (page 28)

Answers may vary.

The internet affects our lives in many ways today. **1** <u>For example</u>, we can communicate with each other by email easily, compared to sending messages by postal mail. **2** <u>Moreover</u>, we can chat with our friends, no matter where they are. **3** <u>Also</u>, we can buy whatever we want on the internet, and we do not need to go out to the shops. **4** <u>Finally</u>, we can pay our bills such as electric fee and gas fee, and manage our accounts online. **5** <u>On the other hand/At the same time</u>, the internet has some disadvantages for people. There is too much information on the internet that is not very useful for us, and some information from the internet is not accurate at all. **6** <u>In addition</u>, the internet reduces the interaction of people to some extent. **7** <u>For instance</u>, your friend may just send an email to you instead of visiting you in person. That will decrease the opportunities for you to meet each other face to face. **8** <u>Furthermore</u>, people can just chat at home on the internet rather than going out with their friends. **9** <u>Therefore</u>, while the internet may make our lives more convenient in many ways, the internet also decreases our social interaction and makes our lives more isolated.

Exercise 2.15: Using Transitions for Coherence in an Essay (page 29)

Answers may vary.

Employment and Taxes

<u>Many</u> developing countries face economic problems. Some people claim that the problems are too difficult to solve. There are, **1** <u>however</u>, positive ways to improve the economic situation of countries and promote the lives of their poor people. These must include an increase in job opportunities and a decrease in the amount of taxes. Increasing employment and decreasing taxes will improve the economic situation of a country and reduce the rate of poverty.

2 <u>First</u>, employment is the active engine that keeps a country going. It is the means by which people are able to care for themselves and their families. **3** <u>For example</u>, job opportunities maintain a certain economic security for people and enable them to improve their lives. This means that they can care for their families and be active, contributing citizens. **4** <u>Moreover</u>, jobs are a symbol of independence and self-sufficiency. A person who is self-sufficient does not need the help of governmental social programs like welfare or medical insurance for assistance in his or her life. **5** <u>Therefore</u>, this individual's self-sufficiency would save

127

money for the government. **6** <u>In contrast</u>, unemployment is the negative condition that keeps an economy in an unfavorable and inactive state. Lack of employment is a serious problem for the individual in the sense that he or she will be and will feel dependent and lost. **7** <u>In such a situation</u>, he or she may depend on the government to provide the basic needs for him or her. The government, **8** <u>then</u>, loses resources and money in supporting such a person.

9 <u>Second</u>, another economic aspect that negatively affects a government is high taxes. Most people complain too much about the large amount of taxes they have to pay to the government. They claim that they cannot afford necessities because they find themselves left with little money. They cannot save money for later situations of need because the amount of their taxes is far out of proportion to their income. Taxes which are too great and which put a person in a tight situation badly affect the population and the economy. **10** <u>As a result</u>, some economists assert that there should be low, fair, and balanced tax regulations that take into consideration people's personal financial situations and create opportunities for them to live a better life. **11** <u>Nevertheless</u>, despite economists' strong support of low taxes, it must be emphasized that they do not want taxes to be eliminated altogether. They realize governments must have revenues to use in social services and job creation. Before setting tax levels, governments should provide jobs to enhance people's economic situation. **12** <u>In addition</u>, there should be a fair decision about the amount of taxes to be paid, taking into account the cost of living and the person's ability to pay a certain amount.

13 <u>In summary</u>, high rates of unemployment and high taxes cause economic problems and lead governments into many financial crises. It is only by giving serious consideration to people's financial situations and providing them with jobs that an economy can be improved and stimulated.

Section 3. Patterns of Essay Organization

Exercise 3.1: Ordering a Narrative Paragraph (page 32)

<u>5</u> a. Meanwhile, the campers, who were also excited and had been talking about how much fun the night was going to be, were devastated.

<u>13</u> b. I don't know what the others wished for, but I wished that I would again have as much fun at the next year's camp.

<u>4</u> c. When it rained heavily Wednesday night, the counselors were all upset because they wanted to have a last chance to all be together and have fun.

<u>6</u> d. Thursday morning we found out that that night was going to be one of the best nights for seeing meteor showers.

<u>1</u> e. One of my best memories took place when I was working at a children's summer camp last year.

<u>3</u> f. To help cheer the campers up, the counselors and campers had planned a big bonfire on Thursday and then a star-gazing session afterwards.

<u>9</u> g. After dinner, we and the campers all gathered in a big clearing by the lake and lit the bonfire we had prepared.

<u>2</u> h. It was the last weekend for many of the children at camp and everyone was feeling a bit sad.

<u>12</u> i. For hours, we all watched shooting stars together.

<u>7</u> j. Finding out about the meteor showers made the counselors determined that the bonfire should succeed.

<u>11</u> k. Then, as the bonfire died down, we all brought out our blankets and lay down to look at the stars.

<u>8</u> l. The counselors were inspired to search all day for dry wood and set it up for the bonfire in the evening.

<u>10</u> m. We all sang songs and roasted marshmallows, enjoying how the fire lit up the night.

Exercise 3.2: Practice with *When* and *While* (page 34)

1. <u>When/while</u> he was a junior in college, he met his future wife.
2. We were just leaving the baseball field <u>when</u> a tornado struck.
3. <u>When/while</u> I was watching TV, my brother came home from football practice.
4. <u>When</u> they learned that their daughter had been in an accident, they immediately rushed to the hospital.
5. <u>When</u> I was young, I used to spend a lot of time at my grandparents. I have fond memories of Sunday mornings spent reading the comics section with my grandfather <u>while</u> my grandmother baked homemade bread. To this day, <u>whenever/when</u> I smell freshly baked bread, I think of those happy times.
6. I had asked my neighbor many times not to play loud music in the afternoon <u>when/while</u> my baby was sleeping, but he would not stop. <u>When</u> I just couldn't take it anymore, I finally had to complain to the building manager.
7. At camp, since I didn't like to swim, I would help prepare lunch <u>while</u> the other campers were enjoying swimming in the lake.

8. Do you remember a day <u>when</u> you were so happy you wished that day could last forever?

Exercise 3.3: Practice with Process Words and Phrases (page 35)

How to Find a Doctor

Choosing a physician who will oversee your healthcare can be a difficult decision, but the process can be made less stressful by following a few simple steps. It is important to work through this process before you urgently need healthcare, so that you can make a wise and carefully thought-out decision. <u>An initial step</u> in this process is to ask friends for recommendations. Although your experience with a particular doctor may differ from another person's, these opinions can be very valuable in helping you to narrow your search to just a few doctors. <u>Once</u> you have a list of several doctors for whom you have received personal recommendations, you should call each office to ask a few questions: Is the practice accepting new patients? Can the doctor address your (or your family's) particular health concerns? You should also note whether the staff seem professional and friendly. <u>Another very important step</u> in this process is to find out whether your insurance company will cover visits to the physician that you select. You should check with both your insurance company and the doctor's office to verify this. If the answers to your initial questions are positive, a <u>subsequent</u> but optional <u>step</u> is to visit the office in person. Besides determining the convenience of the location, you can observe the atmosphere of the waiting room and examination rooms, and the personalities and mannerisms of the office staff and nurses. A visit also gives you the opportunity to interview the physician and ascertain his or her personality and approach to healthcare. <u>To complete the process</u> of selecting a doctor, you should inform both the doctor's office and your insurance company of your decision, so that there are no delays or complications when the time comes for you and your family to rely on your doctor's expertise.

Exercise 3.4: Connecting Ideas Using Process Words and Phrases (page 36)

Answers will vary.

Exercise 3.5: Connecting Ideas Using Comparison/Contrast Words and Phrases (page 37)

Answers will vary.

1. *online shopping / shopping in a store*
   a. <u>Similar to</u> online shopping, shopping in a store can be a frustrating experience.
   b. Shopping in a store requires you to spend time and money to get to a physical location. Online shopping<u>, on the other hand,</u> is more convenient in that you don't have to leave your house to buy something you want or need.

2. *older people / younger people*
   a. Older people sometimes struggle to understand the behavior of younger people. <u>Similarly,</u> younger people sometimes struggle to understand the behavior of older people.
   b. Older people and younger people <u>differ with respect to</u> their ability to use new technology easily.

3. *fast food restaurant / sit-down restaurant*
   a. Fast food restaurants and sit-down restaurants <u>are similar</u> in that both save you the time and trouble of having to make a meal yourself.
   b. Fast food restaurants serve many foods high in fat and calories. <u>However,</u> at a sit-down restaurant, the menu is generally bigger and you can find more choices for healthier options.

4. *Spending time looking at your friends' social media accounts / spending time with your friends in person*
   a. <u>Like</u> spending time with your friends in person, spending time looking at your friends' social media accounts allows you to discover what activities they have been doing lately.
   b. <u>Nonetheless,</u> because people generally post only what they want other to see, you are not getting the whole picture when you look at your friends' social media accounts.

5. *tropical climate / temperate climate*
   a. <u>Both</u> a tropical climate <u>and</u> a temperate climate offer wonderful landscapes.
   b. <u>Whereas</u> tropical climates are often hot and humid, temperate climates have more moderate temperatures and lower humidity levels in genera.

Exercise 3.6: Using Comparison/Contrast Words to Create a Paragraph (page 38)

Answers will vary.

Exercise 3.7: Identifying Cause-and-Effect Words and Phrases
(page 39)

The Changing of the World with the Advent of the Internet

Imagine life before the internet. People waited in long lines to pay bills at banks. At the beginning of the semester, college offices were filled with students who wanted to register for their classes. When you couldn't find something in one store, you would have to drive to many others looking for it and perhaps just have to do without. Clearly, even though only a few decades have passed since the internet started to become commonly used, we can realize that the internet contributed to great changes in many parts of our lives.

First of all, the most important effect of the internet has been to increase accessibility of information. The internet allows people to get information easily, no matter the place or time. People do not need to go to the library and read several books to get information. That is because Google, the most popular web search engine, can show the web pages containing information people are searching within just a few seconds. Likewise, conventional encyclopedias in the library are not used so much any more because most people use Wikipedia, one of the biggest information providers on the internet. Thus, most students, researchers, and even common people would be very inconvenienced if the internet were no longer available. This demonstrates the important position the internet holds in our daily lives.

In addition, the internet has had an impact on facilitating interpersonal communication. For supporting examples one need look no further than email. Today, most students and workers turn on their computer in the morning and check email first. To send and receive email takes less than one minute. Many international students also use apps to talk with their family at any time or place. This definitely has resulted in positive outcomes for international students, who are far from home and may be feeling lonely due to culture shock. The fact that these students can easily communicate with their friends and family abroad leads to a sense of community and well-being that may help them through their period of culture shock.

Moreover, online shopping has become quite popular due to the ease with which you can order items from almost any store. Sites like Amazon have sprung up to meet customers' desire to receive what they want as quickly as possible and as cheaply as possible. Because customers do not need to drive to a store, they can save time as well as money. This is another way in which the internet has greatly affected our lives.

Finally, the most striking <u>effect</u> of the internet has been the advent of online services. Today, people use many kinds of online services. People often pay bills using online banking. Students tend to register for classes or hand in their homework online. Many governments provide online services including registration for the driver's test and photo ID to shorten citizens' waiting time at the office. <u>Because</u> it is so simple, using online services has become part of our daily lives as well, and the internet is the phenomenon that has made it possible.

The internet <u>has</u> greatly <u>affected</u> our lives. It helps us access information easily any place or time. We can communicate with those who live very far away using email and some websites allow us to shop at less cost and in less time. Furthermore, not only online shopping but also online services allow us to <u>decrease</u> the effort it takes to go to the store, bank, and government offices. Our lives have gradually changed due to the internet so that now we might even say it has become a necessity!

Exercise 3.8: Connecting Ideas Using Cause-and-Effect Words and Phrases (page 41)

In the U.S. the divorce rate continues to rise every year. **1** <u>One reason for</u> this constant increase is the fact that divorces have become so common. Before the 1980s, divorced people were not viewed as the norm. The commonly accepted belief was that these people should have tried harder to work out their marital difficulties. Now, however, **2** <u>as</u> such a high percentage of married people get divorced, it may seem like a normal part of life. With more than 50% of marriages in the U.S. eventually ending in divorce, no one can take the attitude that divorced people are "strange." In addition, **3** <u>because</u> there is no longer a social taboo against getting a divorce, people do not feel compelled to "stick it out." **4** <u>This has resulted in</u> a situation in which couples may go into a marriage thinking, "If it doesn't work out, I can always get a divorce." A typical **5** <u>consequence</u> of this kind of thinking is that when a difficult problem arises, rather than working hard to solve it or accepting that a compromise might be the only way to solve the problem, the couple uses divorce as a solution.

Exercise 3.9: Identifying Argument Words and Phrases (page 42)

Early Computer Education: Its Negative Effects on the Intellectual Development of Children

Imagine a group of kindergarten students sitting in front of their screens in the computer room of an elementary school. They look into the dazzling images on their individually assigned computer screen while hardly talking to each other. No smile or liveliness can be found in this room, where these 6-year-old children start learning how to adapt themselves to the so-called age of information technology. Even though the computer is now an essential part of modern life, it doesn't seem logical to waste valuable childhood hours on a computer when children should be performing creative activities and discovering life for themselves. In fact, <u>many people argue that</u> computer education in early elementary years has several negative effects on the intellectual development of children: lowering their concentration on a task, preventing them from acquiring social skills, and exposing them to a hazardous online environment.

First of all, early computer education can lower children's concentration on a task. While young children learn on the computer, they use lots of software or computer games which contain attractive images. Even though they seem to pay attention to the work on the computer, actually they are just looking at the monitor, overwhelmed by the glittering pictures. This strong visual stimulation irritates children's minds and the children are apt to lose interest in things without such a dazzling display. To them, <u>it may seem</u> boring and dumb to read a storybook because it is not moving fast or shining with bright images. As a result, children can be easily distracted and cannot concentrate on the important tasks for their ages such as reading books, writing their opinions, or solving logical problems, which are definitely needed for their academic success and mental growth. <u>We can deduce that this will lead to</u> problems for the children later in life when these skills are necessary.

Another negative effect of early computer education is that children lose time and opportunity to socialize with peers. Because most children tend to work on the computer alone for a long time, they confine themselves in virtual space and are reluctant to interact with peers. Even though they need lots of social experiences in early childhood to grow into a well-rounded person, children can be easily involved in computer activity and may spend all of their free time doing something on the computer. <u>Consequently</u>, they are deprived of important opportunities to play and talk with their friends. <u>It is reasonable to assume</u>, then, that in this type of situation, where children grow up into adults without sufficient opportunity to interact with peers, they may have less of a capability to participate in our complex and interactive society.

Finally, children can be exposed to the hazardous online environment. For example, there is a great deal of inappropriate material on the internet like pornography, violence, and hatred. Those things exert a very bad influence on children. Because children are so sensitive and do not have much knowledge of life, they accept the dangerous influences as reality. In addition, they can encounter bullies or molesters via chatting or email. Due to the anonymity, a criminal can easily approach the innocent children and lure them into a very harmful situation. Therefore, children may experience physical danger as well.

In conclusion, early computer education may have a negative impact on children with respect to the development of concentration and social skills and to the possibility of harmful internet experiences. Therefore, it is better to teach children how to use a computer in their later elementary grades, taking into consideration their developmental stages. In doing this, we will be able to minimize the negative effects of children's computer education.

Exercise 3.10: Connecting Ideas Using Logical Argument (page 44)

Answers will vary.

Exercise 3.11: Making Generalizations (page 45)

Answers may vary.

1. Heesung, Maria, and Abdullah are all students in Professor Huang's engineering class. Heesung has recently won an award for her research. Maria has a scholarship to study at the university for two years. Abdullah has been elected president of the Student Engineering Organization.
    Professor Huang must be a very good teacher.

2. Akiko Yokohama has studied French for nine years. Her brother, Taro, works as a translator for a financial company in Germany. Their mother teaches English at a school in Tokyo.
    Members of the Yokohama family have a talent for learning languages.

3. In Hunter's Woods, 25 murders took place last year. There were also 53 cases of robbery and 10 drive-by shootings.
    The city of Hunter's Woods must be a dangerous place.

4. Colleges are using online systems for grading. They are also using online systems for posting syllabi and offering orientation information online.

Colleges <u>are taking full advantage of the information sharing capabilities of the internet.</u>

5. Parents use lullabies to help put their babies to sleep. Many hospitals use music therapy to help their patients feel better. Many people, after coming home from a long day at work, put some music on to help them relax. *Music* <u>can help calm people of all ages.</u>

Section 4. Research Paper

Exercise 4.1: Evaluating Sources (page 48)

Answers will vary.

Exercise 4.2: Summarizing (page 51)

Answers will vary

Exercise 4.3: Recognizing Plagiarism (page 54)

1. B
2. C
3. A
4. D
5. B
6. B
7. E
8. D
9. C
10. A
11. E
12. B
13. D
14. A
15. C
16. D

Exercise 4.4: Ordering Outline Headings (page 59)

Title: *The Benefits of Participating in a Study Group*
Main Idea: <u>Several benefits to participating in a study group</u>

1. Get a support system
   a. Have someone to ask if you don't understand something in class
   b. Can contact someone in the group to get notes if you miss a class
2. Understand the subject better
   a. Get new perspectives from discussion with other students
   b. Helps you think more deeply about the topic you are studying
3. Can see how others study
   a. Learn new study skills
   b. Can practice new study skills in a group setting

Exercise 4.5: Thesis Statements: Argument or Report? (page 60)

1. R
2. A (Keywords: <u>although</u>, <u>must</u>)
3. R
4. A (Keywords: <u>however</u>, <u>should</u>)
5. R
6. A (Keywords: <u>need to</u>)
7. R
8. A (Keywords: <u>must</u>)
9. R
10. A (Keywords: <u>best</u>)

Exercise 4.6: APA References: Correcting Errors (page 61)

1. Book

Loy, M. (2023). *Connecting communities in archaic Greece: Exploring economic and political networks through data modelling*. Cambridge University Press.

2. Book

Salesh, B., & Jounell, G. (2017). *Giving up technology may just make your day* (2nd ed.). University of Chicago Press.

3. Edited book

Concueso, L. (Ed). (2016). *Critical thinking: A collection of essays*. Stanford, CA: Stanford University Press.

4. Journal article

O'Toole, R.S. (2017). The bonds of kinship, the ties of freedom in colonial Peru. *Journal of family history* 42(1), 3–21.

5. Chapter in an edited book

Neruda, P. (2017). If you forget me. In M. Strand (Ed.), *100 great poems of the twentieth century* (pp. 21–22). ~~New York, NY:~~ W.W. Norton & Company.

6. Newspaper article

Maloney, J. (2024, June 10). U.S. pledges crackdown on illegal e-cigarettes. *The Wall Street Journal.* https://www.wsj.com/health/u-s-pledges-crackdown-on-illegal-e-cigarettes-2bf20794?mod=hp_lead_pos6

7. Book

Krawec, P. (2022). *Becoming kin: An indigenous call to unforgetting the past and reimagining our future.* Broadleaf Books.

8. Journal article

Buxton, R. & Draper, J. (2022). Refugees, membership, and state system legitimacy. *Ethics & Global Politics, 15(4)*, 113–130. https://doi.org/10.1080/16544951.2022.2151286

Exercise 4.7: MLA Works Cited: Correcting Errors (page 62)

1. Book

deGrasse Tyson, Neil. *Cosmic Queries: StarTalk's Guide to Who We Are, How We Got Here, and Where We're Going.* National Geographic, 2021.

2. Book

Springfield, Janice, and Simone Manchester. *A History of Immigrants in the US.* W.W. Norton and Company, 2012.

3. Chapter in an edited volume

Kendal, Dave, Emily Minor, and Monika Egerer. "People's Decisions Shape Urban Habitats." *Routledge Handbook of Urban Biodiversity,* edited by Charles H. Nilon and Myla F.J. Aronson ~~(Eds.)~~, Routledge, 2024, pp. 111–26.

4. Journal article

Martinez-Austria, Polioptro F., and Erick R. Bandala. "Temperature and Heat-Related Mortality Trends in the Sonoran and Mojave Desert Region." *Atmosphere,* vol. 8, no. 3, 2017, pp.1–13.

5. Journal article

Maheux, Anne, et al. "Grateful: Longitudinal Associations Between Adolescents' Social Media Use and Gratitude During the COVID-19 Pandemic." *Journal of Research on Adolescence,* vol. 31, no. 3, 2021, pp. 734–47.

6. Newspaper article

Kevany, Sophie. "Wild Horses Return to Kazakhstan Steppes After Absence of Two Centuries." *The Guardian*, 10 June 2024. https://www.theguardian.com/environment/article/2024/jun/10/przewalskis-horses-only-wild-species-return-central-asian-steppes-kazakhstan.

7. Edited book

Gonzales, Laura, and Michelle Hall Kells, editors. *Latina Leadership: Language and Literacy Education across Communities.* Syracuse University Press, 2022.

8. Book

Pevar, Stephen L. *The Rights of Indians and Tribes.* 5th ed., Oxford University Press, 2024.

Exercise 4.8: Chicago Works Cited: Correcting Errors (page 64)

1. Book

Petcoff, Omonpee W., Janice C. Palaganas, and Marcel Danesi. *Emoji in Higher Education: A Healthcare-Based Perspective.* Cambridge: Cambridge University Press, 2024.

2. Book

Deaton, Angus. *The Great Escape: Health, Wealth, and the Origins of Inequality.* Princeton, NJ: Princeton University Press, 2024.

3. Journal article

Sakeeny, Matt. "Textures of Black Sound and Affect: Life and Death in New Orleans." *American Anthropologist 126,* no. 2 (2024): 295–310.

4. Chapter in an edited book

Silver, Blake R., and Graziella Pagliarulo McCarron. "Understanding College Students of Immigrant Origin." In *Supporting College Students of Immigrant Origin: New Insights from Research, Policy, and Practice,* edited by Blake R. Silver and Graziella Pagliarulo McCarron, pp. 3–16. Cambridge: Cambridge University Press, 2024.

Exercise 4.9: IEEE Works Cited: Correcting Errors (page 65)

1. Book

[1] N. Gredecki and P. Turner, Eds. *Forensic Psychology.* New York, NY, USA: Routledge, 2022.

139

2. Journal article

[2] A. V. Kaplienko, B. A. Gabaraev, and Y. S. Cherepnin, "Potential role of nuclear power in a carbon-free world," *Nuclear Energy and Technology,* vol. 10, no. 2, pp. 89–96, 2024.

3. Journal article

[3] K. Olobatuyi, M.R.P. Parker, and O. Ariyo, "Cluster weighted model based on TSNE algorithm for high-dimensional data," *International journal of Data Science and Analytics,* vol. 17, no. 3, pp. 261–273, 2024.

4. Chapter in an edited book

[4] E. C. Carroll, "Beyond the watchdog: Using law to build trust in the press," in *Media and Society After Technological Disruption,* K. Langvardt and J. Hurwitz, Eds. Cambridge: Cambridge University Press, 2024, pp. 47–60.

Section 5. Grammar and Style

Exercise 5.1: Word Form Errors (page 68)

1. The lens acted as a prism, making the light <u>look</u> like a rainbow.
2. Most of the <u>mice</u> were used as control in the experiment.
3. The most <u>commonly</u> used material for computer <u>keyboards</u> is a type of polymer.
4. Historically, <u>wars</u> are often fought because political entities decide they <u>want</u> more land or resources.
5. The shipping of <u>supplies</u> from the factory is usually done on Mondays and Wednesdays.
6. By law, families must use car seats for all <u>children</u> eight years old or younger.
7. After the invited speaker finished <u>talking</u>, she took <u>questions</u> from the audience.
8. It is important to be <u>diplomatic</u> when dealing with a matter involving the development of a peace treaty among nations.
9. At the library you can find many different <u>types</u> of books.
10. Before <u>writing</u> the paper, students should <u>make</u> an outline.

Exercise 5.2: Word Forms (page 69)

1. After <u>visiting</u> his brother, Paul drove to Toronto.
2. Three <u>women</u> applied for the open position in the Sociology department.

3. In order to cook noodles, first you need <u>to boil</u> a pot of water.
4. The architect showed us several different <u>designs</u> for the entrance.
5. I was confused because the grocery store had been <u>remodeled</u> and the produce <u>was</u> in a different location.
6. When we were standing next to it, the wind turbine was <u>surprisingly</u> tall.
7. They did not see any other <u>bicycles</u> while they were riding on the trail.
8. Physics <u>is</u> one of her favorite <u>subjects</u> in school.
9. The little girl sang <u>beautifully</u> in the <u>crowded</u> auditorium.
10. You should <u>research</u> carefully before <u>buying</u> a car.

Exercise 5.3: Articles (page 70)

My hobby is oil painting. I often go to **1** <u>the</u> museum to look at **2** <u>0</u> various paintings. Among **3** <u>the</u> artists on display at the museum, I prefer Maurice Utrillo, **4** <u>a</u> French painter who mainly drew Montmartre in Paris. Utrillo had three phases in his painting life: **5** <u>the</u> "montagny period," **6** <u>the</u> "colorist period," and **7** <u>the</u> "white period." I prefer **8** <u>the</u> paintings from the last phase. **9** <u>The</u> first paintings he did are only like imitations of **10** <u>the</u> Impressionists, and I find these canvases uninspiring. **11** <u>The</u> paintings from **12** <u>the</u> "colorist period" give us **13** <u>a</u> cheerful impression that is too bright for me. On the other hand, Utrillo's paintings from **14** <u>the</u> "white period" move me deeply. **15** <u>The</u> whitish colors with **16** <u>0</u> muted tones make me feel melancholy and contemplative. In addition, **17** <u>the</u> various tones of whites give me **18** <u>0</u> impressions of loneliness and isolation. I enjoy viewing **19** <u>0</u> Utrillo's paintings alone to feel those moods and emotions that only he gives us through his "white period," and when I paint **20** <u>0</u> pictures, I often imitate these tones because I wish to create **21** <u>a</u> similar melancholy feeling.

Exercise 5.4: Articles (page 71)

1. Hallway <u>walls</u> need to be painted every two or three <u>years</u>.
   Explanation:
   <u>hallway walls: non-specific/general (no article)</u>
   <u>two or three years: number replaces article (no article)</u>
2. The <u>letter</u> that I just received is from an old <u>friend</u>.
   Explanation:
   <u>the letter: specific object (defined in the sentence)</u>
   <u>an old friend: one of several (non-specific)</u>

3. I bought <u>coffee</u> from the <u>Starbucks</u> in the <u>student union</u>.

Explanation:

<u>coffee: non-count noun (no article)</u>

<u>the Starbucks: specific location</u>

<u>the student union: specific location</u>

4. You can sometimes find examples of Early American <u>furniture</u> in <u>museums</u>.

Explanation:

<u>furniture: non-count noun (no article)</u>

<u>museums: non-specific/general group (no article)</u>

5. <u>Universities</u> often have <u>libraries</u> with <u>special collections</u>.

Explanation:

<u>universities: non-specific/general group (no article)</u>

<u>libraries: non-specific/general group (no article)</u>

<u>special collections: non-specific/general group (no article)</u>

Exercise 5.5: Looking at Nouns in Context to Determine Article Use (page 72)

1 I remember one <u>day</u> when I was traveling to another <u>city</u> by <u>train</u>.

<u>one day—general quantifier "one" in place of article</u>

<u>city—determiner ("another") in place of article</u>

<u>train—no article: general category</u>

2 The <u>journey</u> was very long.

<u>the journey—specific (identified previously)</u>

3 Sitting next to me there was a <u>family</u> who had annoying and unbearable <u>children</u>.

<u>a family—non-specific and singular</u>

<u>children—no article: non-specific and plural</u>

4 It was a long and frustrating <u>day</u> for me.

<u>a…day—non-specific and singular</u>

5 I had to bear the <u>noise</u> and <u>misbehavior</u> of the <u>children</u>.

<u>the noise—specific (defined by "of…")</u>

<u>the misbehavior—specific (defined by "of…")</u>

<u>the children—specific (identified earlier)</u>

6 I know that <u>children</u> make <u>noise</u>.

<u>children—no article: general category</u>

<u>noise—no article: non-count</u>

7   They go through a very energetic <u>phase</u> that is part of <u>life</u>.

<u>a...phase—non-specific and singular</u>

<u>life—no article: non-count</u>

8   That's their <u>job</u>.

<u>job—possessive ("their") in place of article</u>

9   The <u>children</u> were only being <u>children</u>, doing what <u>children</u> do.

<u>the children—specific (identified earlier)</u>

<u>children—no article: general category</u>

<u>children—no article: general category</u>

10 However, there is a <u>limit</u> to everything.

<u>a limit—non-specific and singular</u>

11 Those <u>children</u> went far beyond the <u>limit</u>.

<u>children—demonstrative ("those") in place of article</u>

<u>the limit—specific (mentioned earlier)</u>

12 As a <u>passenger</u>, I am entitled to have a peaceful and quiet <u>environment</u> when traveling.

<u>a passenger—non-specific and singular</u>

<u>a...environment—non-specific and singular</u>

13 These <u>parents</u> should have worked harder to help their <u>children</u> to be quiet.

<u>parents—demonstrative ("these") in place of article</u>

<u>children—possessive ("their") in place of article</u>

14 Before taking a long <u>trip</u>, <u>parents</u> should teach their <u>children</u> how to behave in a public <u>place</u> or when using public <u>transportation</u>.

<u>a...trip—non-specific and singular</u>

<u>parents—no article: non-specific and plural</u>

<u>children—possessive ("their") in place of article</u>

<u>a...place—non-specific and singular</u>

<u>transportation—no article: non-count</u>

15 In this way, neither the <u>passengers</u> nor the <u>parents</u> would have a hard <u>time</u> on their <u>trip</u>, and everybody would be relaxed, especially me!

<u>the passengers—specific group</u>

<u>the parents—specific group</u>

<u>a...time—non-specific and singular</u>

<u>trip—possessive ("their") in place of article</u>

Exercise 5.6: Articles (page 73)

In **1** the [specific country with a countable noun in its name] United States, high levels of competition can affect **2** 0 [general] social relationships among youth and adults, leading **3** 0 [general] people to consider themselves as single individuals who should be ready to achieve their personal goals instead of being cooperative. Sometimes **4** 0 [non-count / general] competitiveness prevents young people from just enjoying their activities; they forget that **5** the [specified by "of..."] primary purpose of **6** 0 [non-count] sports, music, and education is to enrich our lives and to teach us how to live in our society. It is **7** a [general] problem because **8** 0 [general] people are just focused on themselves. A major difference between **9** the [specified by "of..."] values of the United States and my country, Venezuela, is that we don't believe as much as Americans in **10** 0 [non-count] competition. We believe more in cooperation with each other. **11** An [non-specific] example is that in America to find **12** a [non-specific] job you need excellent skills and abilities to stand out from the rest of **13** the [specific group] potential employees. However, in Venezuela you just need to know people—the more contacts and more friends you have, the better. That is **14** the [specified by "of..."] culture of finding **15** a [non-specific] job in my country. Having **16** a [non-specific] friend or **17** a [non-specific] family member is what is going to increase the chances of getting **18** 0 [non-count] employment. This shows how much we value **19** 0 [general] relationships in my country, but it can be **20** a [non-specific] drawback because Venezuelans are more prepared to be friendly than to strive to be **21** the [specific / superlative] best.

Exercise 5.7: Prepositions (page 74)

I did haircuts **1** for some friends recently, and I realized the process of hair-cutting is similar **2** to the writing process. When you start to cut hair for somebody, you need to figure **3** out the best style for this person, so you consult **4** with her or him, give some suggestions, and get some feedback. This is the same as generating ideas **5** for writing. Next you start cutting the hair **6** in the shape you designed. **7** At this stage, you don't work **8** on the details, but rather cut the hair **9** in each area such that you get a basic style. This phase compares **10** to drafting in writing. As you go on, you may find that the hairstyle you designed first is not good enough **11** in some ways. Therefore, you need to change it to fit the shape **12** of the person's face. Revising for writing is the same. Although this phase is similar for both hair-cutting and writing, there is a little difference **13** between them.

In writing, you can delete some paragraphs and write new ones, but in hair-cutting you cannot put **14** <u>back</u> the hair that you have cut **15** <u>off</u>. Last, when you are happy **16** <u>with</u> the shape and style of the haircut, you need to work **17** <u>on</u> some details, similar to the final editing stage in writing. You can smooth the edges **18** <u>of</u> the hair, or put some gel **19** <u>in/on</u> it, while in your essay you may want to check the spelling, punctuation, citations, or bibliography. After this, you can step back and admire your good work!

Exercise 5.8: Prepositions (page 75)

A Language of Wider Communication (LWC) is any language that allows communication **1** <u>among / between</u> speakers of different languages, either **2** <u>within</u> a single country or across national boundaries. In many countries, education is usually provided in the country's LWC, and the national LWC is generally used **3** <u>within / in</u> systems of government.

An LWC may be a language native to the region **4** <u>in</u> which it is used (such as Tok Pisin in Papua New Guinea), but this is not necessarily the case (as with English in many countries). Sometimes a country uses an LWC that is a local or regional language, not a major world language, which eases communication **5** <u>among</u> citizens of that country and enhances the sense of national identity. This is the case **6** <u>for / in</u> Uzbekistan, for example, where the official language (and LWC) is Uzbek, which is not widely spoken **7** <u>outside</u> of that country. Other countries may select the language **8** <u>of</u> former colonizers as the national LWC, as did many of the former French colonies in Africa. This choice allows for easier communication **9** <u>across</u> national borders with other people who share the same LWC.

Exercise 5.9: Phrasal Verbs (page 76)

1. In his answer, Maurice <u>mixed up</u> two theories that should have been kept separate.
    In his answer, Maurice *confused* two theories that should have been kept separate.
2. Katherine can't <u>put up with</u> people who act in a superior manner.
    Katherine can't *tolerate* people who act in a superior manner.
3. We must carefully <u>break down</u> the components of this problem before we can find a solution.
    We must carefully *analyze* the components of this problem before we can find a solution.

4. When Anna <u>gets through with</u> the first project, she will immediately start the next one.

When Anna *finishes* the first project, she will immediately start the next one.

5. The dietician told me that I must <u>cut down on</u> my salt intake.

The dietician told me that I must *reduce* my salt intake.

6. Octavia must <u>keep on</u> studying hard if she wants to pass the test.

Octavia must *continue* studying hard if she wants to pass the test.

7. Professor Benatar <u>found out</u> why the volcano was emitting lava.

Professor Benatar *discovered* why the volcano was emitting lava.

8. Leo <u>threw away</u> the damaged equipment.

Leo *discarded* the damaged equipment.

9. The data indicate that the temperatures <u>go up and down</u> a great deal.

The data indicate that the temperatures *fluctuate* a great deal.

10. Due to bad weather, we had to <u>call off</u> our field trip to the science center.

Due to bad weather, we had to *cancel* our field trip to the science center.

Exercise 5.10: Phrasal Verbs (page 78)

Answers may vary.

There are several factors to **1** ~~think about~~ <u>consider</u> when choosing a major or career. First, when a hobby **2** ~~turns into~~ <u>becomes</u> a profession it places a financial burden on that job that might make people less passionate about it. Moreover, sometimes people **3** ~~find out~~ <u>discover</u> that something they love to do as a hobby does not provide enough income for them to be financially stable. People who **4** ~~look forward to~~ <u>anticipate</u> their hobby being their sole source of income may **5** ~~end up~~ <u>become</u> frustrated and discouraged when they realize this may be impossible. Even if it is not the primary thing that they love to do, someone can feel fulfilled by their job; in fact, they can likely both find satisfaction in their work and **6** ~~set aside~~ <u>dedicate</u> time for their hobbies. People can surely **7** ~~come across~~ <u>encounter</u> opportunities to pursue their passion outside of work. Students need to carefully **8** ~~think about~~ <u>consider</u> these points when **9** ~~picking out~~ <u>selecting</u> a major and a future career. Then they can **10** ~~figure out~~ <u>discern</u> what is really the best path for them.

Exercise 5.11: Word Choice (page 79)

This short essay includes a variety of informal and general words, some of which have been underlined. There may be additional words that you think are general and/or informal. Replace these words with more formal or specific words. Be prepared to discuss your answers. Some word changes may require changing the sentence structure or adding a longer noun phrase. Answers may vary.

When I left my country and moved away from my family, I needed to learn new ~~things~~ skills. For example, I was ~~awful~~ unskilled at cooking before I came here, but now I am a ~~good~~ competent cook. Furthermore, I eat ~~proper~~ nutritious food and pay more attention to what I eat because if I get sick, nobody will take care of me. Although I do not have ~~lots of~~ abundant time to spend on eating and cooking, I still insist on eating regularly and at home.

Another effect of leaving my family is having to manage ~~everything~~ my time and money ~~better~~ more thoughtfully and without help. For instance, I have more time than before, and I can decide how to spend it. I do not need to ~~get~~ seek permission to do anything. I have ~~made~~ created a study schedule for myself and have been following it day by day. Moreover, it has already ~~taken~~ cost my parents ~~lots of~~ a great deal of money to ~~let~~ allow me to study here. Thus, I should manage my money ~~well~~ carefully by not buying luxury ~~things~~ items, by comparing prices, and by using discounts when I make purchases.

Finally, leaving my family and living by myself has been ~~good~~ beneficial for me because it made me ~~grow up~~ mature fast and ~~get~~ acquire a sense of independence. It is very difficult for me to get used to this kind of life. Some ~~things~~ aspects have changed and are different from before, such as my diet and my time and money management. However, I think I am ~~getting~~ receiving an important and helpful learning experience for my whole life. Such experiences are ~~good~~ valuable for all people.

Exercise 5.12: Reference Words (page 80)

Answers may vary.

1. Professor Lee told Professor Dodd that her students were hard workers.
   <u>Professor Lee thought that Professor Dodd's students were hard workers, and she told Professor Dodd so.</u>

2. If the nations of the world all agreed to apply the same policies, they would be more successful.

The nations of the world would all be more successful if they could agree to apply the same policies.

3. Athletics at the Olympic level requires dedicated daily training. They actually spend years of their lives working towards this goal.
Athletes spend years of their lives in dedicated daily training, working toward the goal of competing at the Olympic level.

4. Several political campaigns were affected by unexpected global conflicts. The conflicts changed the way that voters viewed the candidates' positions.
Several political campaigns were affected by unexpected global conflicts, which changed the way that voters viewed the candidates' positions.

5. Maria told me that there were two ways to interpret the experiment's results: one was that it was a well-conducted experiment and another was that its design was weak. I had not previously thought it was an issue.
Maria told me that there were two ways to interpret the experiment's results: one was that it was a well-conducted experiment and another was that its design was weak. I had not previously thought that the design was an issue.

6. The diplomats have refused to negotiate a ceasefire agreement, which is not acceptable.
The diplomats' refusal to negotiate a ceasefire agreement is not acceptable.

7. The factory managers told the other employees that they would be getting an increase in their pay.
The employees will be getting an increase in their pay, according to the factory managers.

8. We emailed the office of the daily newspaper about the latest news, but it did not reply.
We did not receive a reply after emailing the office of the daily newspaper about the latest news.

9. The typical romantic movie, it presents an unreal view of life.
This film—a typical romantic movie—presents an unreal view of life.

10. Because of living there for a long time, Miguel said that I should be able to speak Spanish fluently.
Miguel said that I should be able to speak Spanish fluently, since I had lived there for a long time.

Exercise 5.13: Reducing Wordiness in Sentences (page 81)

Answers may vary.

1. Tyrone's argument is not very persuasive because it is a weak argument that provides little evidence to show that it is valid.

   <u>Tyrone's argument provides little evidence and is therefore not very persuasive.</u>

2. After reading her report, we decided that the hiring policy regarding new workers should not be applied in our consideration of the hiring of anyone new.

   <u>After reading her report, we decided that the hiring policy should not apply to future applicants.</u>

3. If economists were to base their recommendations only on the data they receive from corporations, their recommendations would not be based on enough information to give good advice.

   <u>Economists would be unable to provide good advice if they were to base their recommendations only on the data they receive from corporations.</u>

4. It is the opinion of Ms. MacDonald that we should not support any politicians who promise that everything will become perfect in the future if we vote for them.

   <u>Ms. MacDonald does not support politicians who make unrealistic campaign promises.</u>

5. From my viewpoint, study skills are very important skills that we can acquire that will help us when we are studying in school or college to advance our education.

   <u>I believe that study skills are very important in our efforts to advance our education.</u>

Exercise 5.14: Reducing Wordiness in a Paragraph (page 82)

Answers may vary.

These days there are many people exhibiting different types of behavior. Usually people's attitudes in a society and their behavior toward each other and society depend on the education and training they received from their parents when they were young, and that affects their future and their whole lives later on. Based on my own experience and people's habits in a society, it can be shown that parents influence their children's future. During my childhood, my parents taught me good values, the kind of attitudes that should be adopted socially and in every way, according to each situation of my life. In order to give me some proofs and examples, they also used to put into practice these values whenever it was necessary for them, and I grew up with those kinds of attitudes. They taught me honesty, integrity, and courtesy toward all.

<u>People exhibit a wide variety of social behaviors, which often come from the training they received from their parents. During my childhood, I saw my parents put into practice many good values that apply to many aspects of my life. They taught me honesty, integrity, and courtesy toward all.</u>

Exercise 5.15: Subject–Verb Agreement (page 83)

I 1. Even though the ~~answer~~ <u>answers</u> are correct, the way in which you got the answer is not clear.

I 2. Each of the 12 questions ~~have~~ <u>has</u> only one correct answer.

C 3. They decided to meet on Thursday to finish writing their programs, which are due on Friday.

C 4. In order to solve these problems, we need to first look at what is causing them.

I 5. Neither my teacher nor my advisor ~~know~~ <u>knows</u> the answer.

C 6. Many of the characters in the novel *The Lord of the Rings* are based on beings from Celtic mythology.

I 7. Both of the societies that we are studying in our textbook right now ~~seems~~ <u>seem</u> to share a common ideological foundation.

C 8. It has been shown that the majority of the population in each of those countries does not vote in the annual election.

I 9. It is difficult to determine whether the parent or the child ~~were~~ <u>was</u> to blame.

I 10. The news these days ~~are~~ <u>is</u> full of stories of violence.

Exercise 5.16: Subject–Verb Agreement (page 84)

Mastering a skill <u>requires</u> [require] many hours of practice and hard work. Some people <u>suggest</u> [suggest] that 10,000 hours of practice <u>is</u> [be] necessary before truly becoming a master in a particular skill. But is 10,000 hours a useful number, or is mastery more a matter of natural talent and dedication? I believe that it's neither skill nor hard work. Very few people <u>reach</u> [reach] elite levels of athletic, musical, intellectual, or artistic achievement. I do not believe that everyone who <u>practices</u> [practice] a skill for more than 10,000 hours will become renowned for their skill. Someone who <u>works</u> [work] hard for many years will certainly be highly skilled in their field. But will they be a master? It is difficult to judge that. My brother, along with several of his friends, <u>has</u> [have] been practicing judo for more than ten years. They are all quite skilled and each of them <u>has</u> [have] competed at the national level. There <u>is</u> [be] no doubt that they have worked quite hard and have achieved a high level of skill in judo. Are they masters in their sport? Have they reached the 10,000-hour mark? A better question may be: Are they pursuing their passion and reaching their full potential while maintaining physical and emotional health? This, rather than a mythical 10,000 hours of practice, <u>is</u> [be] the best way to measure success.

Exercise 5.17: Run-On Sentences and Fragments (page 85)

Answers may vary.

King Louis 14th demanded that artists paint him as a god or mythological person <u>and</u> add more dignity to his portrait. The king was thus depicted wearing clothes of the emperors of ancient Rome and Greece <u>to</u> send a message that he was the legitimate successor of the ancient empires. In these paintings, there were also goddesses and legendary heroes around the king <u>to</u> impress people with his honorable character.

Moreover, the height of the king in paintings was always bigger than his real height. <u>All</u> of the images were made to strengthen the authority of the king and government.

The famous palace of Versailles was designed to represent the authority and the power of the king in the clearest way. In this palace, many bureaucrats and noble families lived around the king, who was the center of the court. <u>The</u> paintings or statues of him, as well as his symbols, were placed everywhere in the palace. People were surrounded by works of art <u>that</u> were well planned to give a particular impression of the king. Therefore, it was difficult for citizens to be indifferent to the existence of the king at this palace.

Exercise 5.18: Fragments (page 86)

In King Louis 14th's era, arts and new technologies were the most important ways of advertising. He and his court encouraged many kinds of arts and technology <u>to</u> represent the power of the king. In the field of art, he established an organization of painters and patronized many artists <u>including</u> famous sculptors and architects. The Académie Française was established at this time, <u>since</u> he wanted scholars to be studying the French language and to be cultivating it. In the field of science, we can say that the establishment of the national astronomical observatory was one of this king's main achievements.

Exercise 5.19: Comma Splices (page 87)

Answers may vary.

Everyone needs smiles! You need a smile, for example, when you feel lonely or blue. When you are happy, it takes no effort to smile because it is already there. However, when you feel down, it is good to smile. <u>How?</u> It is easy. Lift the edges of your lips. You do not need a big smile<u>:</u> just a little lift makes your mind lighter and warmer. I have to say that I do not know why this works<u>;</u> however, I have heard about a relationship between the physical and mental systems. <u>They</u> are interactive<u>:</u> when you are happy, a smile appears on your face. And when you make a smiling face, you can make yourself feel happy. After I heard about this, I tried it<u>—</u>it worked!

Exercise 5.20: Comma Use in Adjective Clauses (page 88)

The liver is the most important organ that is affected by alcohol. The liver,<u>which is the largest organ in the body,</u> removes or detoxifies poisons, germs, and bacteria from the blood, makes protein, and produces immune agents. Although direct damage from alcohol in the liver cells has not been reported, alcohol and its metabolites injure the liver by blocking its normal metabolism of proteins, fats, and carbohydrates. As a consequence, consuming alcohol on a regular basis causes fatty liver, alcoholic hepatitis, and alcoholic liver cirrhosis, <u>which all prevent the normal functioning of the body</u>. In addition, <u>bleeding that cannot be stopped easily</u> develops when the protein-making function of the liver is destroyed. Gallstones, itching, and jaundice,<u>which is the yellowing of the skin and eyes,</u> also result because of deteriorating bile metabolism. If the liver is not able to detoxify poisons from the blood, these toxins accumulate in the blood and finally in the brain. People <u>who have these problems</u> are likely to suffer from personality changes, mental symptoms, coma, and even death.

Exercise 5.21: Parallel Structure (page 89)

Answers may vary.

Governments frequently divert what science produces into war-related uses. The original reason for scientists inventing things is usually to improve technology and <u>to help</u> people live better. For example, <u>airplanes were invented</u> to shorten travel time, and dynamite was developed for people to remove mountains and <u>build houses</u> there more easily. However, governments changed the purpose of those technologies. The airplane <u>was</u> changed into a <u>military transport for equipment or bombs</u>, and <u>dynamite was turned into a killing tool</u> in these bombs. It is true that people spend a lot of money on researching new technology for a better life; however, a lot more money is spent for <u>developing</u> new technology into new weapons.

Exercise 5.22: Combining Sentences (page 90)

Answers may vary.

1. Memory is a vital quality of human thought. Without memory we would not be able to function in our daily activity.
   <u>Without memory we would not be able to function in our daily activity, because memory is a vital quality of human thought.</u>

2. Memory failures do happen frequently. This causes many problems, such as forgetting important information that we studied for an exam.
   <u>Memory failures do happen frequently, which causes many problems, such as forgetting important information that we studied for an exam.</u>

3. When studying for an exam, you can use different techniques to improve how much you remember the important points. You can highlight the points in your textbook with a marker pen. You can write a summary of the important points on file cards. You can recite the important points out loud to yourself.
   <u>When studying for an exam, you can use different techniques to improve how much you remember the important points: you can highlight the points in your textbook with a marker pen, you can write a summary of the important points on file cards, and you can recite the important points out loud to yourself.</u>

4. I make up possible exam questions based on my class notes. It's a study method I learned from my aunt. She was a professor of psychology. This method has always been the most effective one for me.
   <u>Making up possible exam questions based on my class notes is a method that has always been the most effective for me. It's a study method I learned from my aunt, who was a professor of psychology.</u>

5. Study your class notes before a test. Put the notes aside. Then say the main points out loud, as if you are telling someone what they are. It will help you remember them.

   <u>When studying before a test, you will remember the information best if you put the notes aside and then say the main points out loud, as if you are telling someone what they are.</u>

6. I learned a valuable study method from my friend. My friend Andre seems to remember his class notes very well. It helped me a lot.

   <u>My friend Andre seems to remember his class notes very well, and I learned a valuable study method from him that helped me a lot.</u>

7. Andre advised me not to leave my studying until just before a test. He said that I should have shorter study sessions of the same material every day. He had found this approach to be much more effective than trying to remember everything in one long study session.

   <u>Rather than leaving my studying until just before a test, Andre advised me to have shorter study sessions of the same material every day, an approach that is much more effective than trying to remember everything in one long study session.</u>

8. Memory is affected by repetition. Highlight the important points in your textbook. Read them again and again over a period of several days.

   <u>Since memory is affected by repetition, you should highlight the important points in your textbook and read them again and again over a period of several days.</u>

9. Some students use mnemonics to help them remember facts. A mnemonic is a memory aid. A mnemonic can be a made-up word, a verse, or other verbal or visual device.

   <u>Some students use mnemonics—memory aids that can be made-up words, verses, or other verbal or visual devices—to help them remember facts.</u>

10. I found it hard to remember the colors of the rainbow. Then I learned a simple mnemonic that sounds like a person's name. The mnemonic is "Roy G. Biv." It uses the first letter of each color: red, orange, yellow, green, blue, indigo, violet.

    <u>I found it hard to remember the colors of the rainbow until I learned a simple mnemonic that sounds like a person's name—"Roy G. Biv."—which uses the first letter of each color: red, orange, yellow, green, blue, indigo, violet.</u>

Exercise 5.23: Using Specific Structures to Revise Sentences
(page 93)

Answers may vary.

1. I was very unwilling to take the course in trigonometry. I took the course. **[adverb]**

    I unwillingly took the course in trigonometry.

2. During the 1980s Tim Berners-Lee developed the foundation of what we now call the Web with his work on information retrieval from distributed systems. **[passive]**

    During the 1980s, the foundation of what we now call the Web was developed by Tim Berner-Lee in his work on information retrieval from distributed systems.

3. We missed our flight due to Stanley's failure to arrive on time. **[divided sentence]**

    Due to Stanley's failure to arrive on time, we missed our flight.

4. Janae had studied hard for the final examination in her Biology class. She was sure that she would do very well on it. **[dependent clause]**

    Janae had studied hard for the final examination in her Biology class, and therefore she was sure that she would do very well on it.

5. Paulina was encouraged by her good results on the final History exam. She thought that she might take a more advanced course in the next semester. **[participial phrase]**

    Encouraged by her good results on the final History exam, Paulina thought that she might take a more advanced course in the next semester.

6. Alexander Fleming discovered penicillin when he observed that mold would not grow around a bacteria culture that he had unintentionally left uncovered. **[passive]**

    Penicillin was discovered when Alexander Fleming observed that mold would not grow around a bacteria culture that he had unintentionally left uncovered.

7. Alfonso traveled to Ecuador, where his family was still living. He was happy to go there. **[adverb]**

    Alfonso happily traveled to Ecuador, where his family was still living.

8. I did not say "basketball." I said Enrico is very skilled at tennis. **[divided sentence]**

    What I said was that Enrico is very skilled at tennis, not basketball.

9. I wished that I had studied harder for the spelling test. I arrived at school in a state of anxiety. **[participial phrase]**

   Wishing that I had studied harder for the spelling test, I arrived at school in a state of anxiety.

10. It was not easy to develop a new research program to better understand how the sun transmits radiation. Professor Bigelow and her graduate students were successful in their work and published an article about it. **[dependent clause]**

    Although it was not easy to develop a new research program to better understand how the sun transmits radiation, Professor Bigelow and her graduate students were successful in their work and published an article about it.

Exercise 5.24: Creating More Variety in Sentence Structure (page 95)

Answers may vary.

The use of fossil fuels such as coal, natural gas, and oil has increased greatly over the past century, resulting in many negative effects on the environment. Using more ethanol would be better than relying too much on fossil fuels. Ethanol has several advantages, one of which is that it can be made from many common crops, including sugar cane, corn, and wheat. Growing more of these crops can help farmers increase their income. However, these crops are also needed as food for humans and livestock. A difficult choice has to be made sometimes between growing crops for food and growing crops for fuel. Reducing the supply of food crops may cause an increase in food prices. Moreover, many of the world's people are hungry and need these crops as food. However, with a cheaper fuel source, farmers can grow crops more efficiently since they use fuel-powered equipment for planting and reaping crops. Thus, shifting to ethanol may not only benefit the environment, but may increase farmers' production of crops and benefit the global population.

Section 6. Punctuation

Exercise 6.1: Period at End of Sentence: Correcting Run-On Sentences (page 98)

1. Machines can be helpful if you understand them. Some people don't like any machines.

2. When the sun is shining, I go swimming. When it rains, I go swimming too because I love swimming.

3. Monarch butterflies have a very distinctive look. They are a beautiful orange color with black and white markings.

4. I would very much like to travel to foreign countries as soon as possible. Which ones I will go to will not be certain until I determine the costs of air travel.

5. The raw material of statistics is data or numbers. The data are the result of counting or measurement that assigns numbers to objects.

6. Biostatistics focuses only on biological and medical science areas. There are many biostatistics applications in clinical data.

7. Descriptive statistics is organizing and summarizing data to determine what information the data contain. To organize and summarize data, we can use methods such as order array or measuring the central tendency by mean, median, and mode for population or grouped data.

8. Diabetes can be divided into two categories. One type is Insulin Dependent Diabetes and the other is Non-Insulin Dependent Diabetes.

9. It is important to drink enough water to avoid dehydration. Many people do not drink enough water. Doctors recommend 8 glasses a day.

10. There are many problems in the field of global education. Basically, they arise from the fact that so many children do not attend primary school, so more advanced education is not possible.

Exercise 6.2: Period at End of Sentence: Correcting Errors (page 99)

1. Clara looked out to sea. To her left were some ships. Far beyond the ships, she saw some whales and dolphins. She saw only cliffs and crashing waves to her right. She decided then that she would try to find a ship that would accept her as a passenger for the long journey across the ocean. She was determined to cross the Pacific and begin her search.

2. Omar didn't know where he had left his keys. He looked all over the house for them. He couldn't seem to find them in any of the usual places. He had to go to work. He would be late! He realized that maybe they were in an unusual place. He looked under the cushions of the living room sofa and looked under the refrigerator. He spent more than an hour looking for them. Finally, he found them in a plant on the windowsill.

Exercise 6.3: Question Mark and Period (page 100)

The detective sat in his office thinking about the strange events at the time of the crime. These were his thoughts: Who was the second witness? Why had she vanished so quickly? There were many people who wanted to know. He knew that Anne wanted to know. Sally had asked questions about it. Andrew had also made inquiries. James, however, had asked only two questions. He had asked when the crime occurred. He had also asked why it had been committed. That was very strange. Why had James not asked about the second witness? Did he perhaps know where she was? It would probably be a good idea to question James about his movements after the crime.

Exercise 6.4: Exclamation Point for Strong Feeling (page 101)

1. Oh, wow!
2. Did you find the new location easily?
3. The painting was rather unusual, with a turtle shown in a strange mixture of green, blue, pink, and various shades of red.
4. How strange!
5. Who is that man carrying the book?
6. I can't believe I forgot!
7. Are you able to come to the meeting?
8. What an amazing opportunity!

Exercise 6.5: Exclamation Points, Periods, or Question Marks in a Conversation (page 102)

Customer: How much is this pair of shoes?

Clerk: Ninety-nine dollars.

Customer: That's so expensive!

Clerk: Not really, considering what they are made of.

Customer: What are they made of?

Clerk: A special, rare material originally designed for astronauts' boots for use in outer space.

Customer: How amazing! Perhaps I'll buy a pair.

Clerk: Great! What size shoes do you wear?

Customer: Size 12.

Clerk: Oh no! That size is out of stock.

Customer: Oh well. I guess I won't be buying these shoes today.

Exercise 6.6: Comma after Introductory or Transitional Words and Phrases (page 103)

1. It is customary to place a comma after introductory or transitional words and phrases.
2. Remembering all the serious obstacles faced the previous year, Kamila refused to try again.
3. Having gone over the material carefully in study group, Dominique felt ready for the test.
4. As a means of repairing torn cloth, nothing could be better than this special machine.
5. Being a lazy student from my earliest schooldays, I naturally found it hard to pass examinations.
6. Natalie had become fluent and had made many new friends during her semester abroad.
7. After speaking to his bank manager, the wheat farmer was able to get a loan to enable him to continue farming for another year.
8. At the restaurant Ivan and Olga met many journalists whom they had not seen for 15 years.
9. The letters that were addressed to me were finally delivered to the right address.
10. Except for the writing class, my studies at the Language Institute are very easy.
11. Once they understand English comma usage, the students will find all the other marks of punctuation relatively easy.
12. Moreover, it was absolutely impossible for the ambassador to visit the Prime Minister.

Exercise 6.7: Comma after Introductory Clauses (page 104)

1. When winter comes, Kenji hopes to go skiing.
2. He will buy a bag of oranges if he goes to the supermarket.
3. After Oscar's cousin arrives in Tasmania, they will travel together to the north of the island.
4. Very many students agree that the university offers excellent courses.
5. Unless they can travel to an English-speaking country, students must learn the language in their own countries.

6. Students who want to learn English travel to English-speaking countries if they can.

7. Because certain unusual events have occurred, the detectives are investigating the case.

8. Many people do not smoke because it would affect their health.

9. If my phone is broken, I will need to replace it right away.

10. Since it rained all day, we were not able to go to the park.

Exercise 6.8: Comma before Coordinating Conjunctions Linking Independent Clauses (page 105)

1. There has been an increase in the popularity of volleyball, and many more spectators are attending the games.

2. Some of the tennis players were doing special exercises to improve their game, but others were just relaxing in the clubhouse.

3. My cousins did not like golf, nor did they like cricket.

4. Vincent will travel to Uruguay to start a new branch of his business, or he will stay in his country for two more years and then go to Uruguay.

5. My chemistry teacher keeps very busy since he also does a lot of research.

6. They left the house on time, but they were late to the theater because of an accident.

7. Kumiko gave me advice and I succeeded.

8. Coffee was the only drink available at the small cafeteria, so we drank many cups of strong coffee.

9. The research teams in the computer industry always try to find out what the competition is working on, and they then try to bring out similar or better products.

Exercise 6.9: Comma with Lists of Words, Phrases, or Clauses (page 106)

1. Books, papers, bottles, cans, pens, and pencils were lying scattered on the floor of the room.

2. Sonam decided to study economic theory, business administration, personnel management, and computer programming.

3. Jennifer's sister could not decide whether to study art, French, or linguistics.

4. Hassan refused to go to the store because it was raining very hard, because he felt tired, and because there was enough food in the house.

5. If a politician smiles at you, promises you something wonderful, claims to have done many good things, or criticizes his opponents, you can guess that there must be an election soon.

6. Financial advice, loans, and credit cards were all offered by the new bank.

7. The travel advertisement promised an ideal holiday in South America, with visits to Brazil, Paraguay, Argentina, and Chile.

8. The journalist said that all countries need to diversify their energy sources, find more fossil fuels, and conserve fuel supplies in order to ensure that energy resources are adequate.

9. The complaints to the mayor mentioned problems with parking facilities, traffic flow, public transportation, unsafe pedestrian crossings, and special paths for bicycles.

10. Swimming, walking, jogging, and dance are all good forms of exercise for busy students.

Exercise 6.10: Comma with Coordinate Adjectives (page 107)

1. Senator Pulinski is a tough, outspoken critic of the President's foreign policy.

2. A big, fluffy gray cat is always coming into our yard.

3. It was a difficult, bumpy, long, twisting road that led to the farmhouse on the side of the mountain.

4. Yiwen said that her history class was always interesting, very informative, and quite stimulating.

5. Due to a severe system-wide problem with spam and viruses, our company installed a complicated computer protection program on all our machines.

6. Our walk in the woods turned out to be cold, wet, and tiresome instead of the pleasant, relaxing stroll that we had expected.

7. The best exhibit in the art gallery was a ten-foot-wide concrete and metal statue of a horse and rider.

8. The Queen's chefs prepared a delicious, mildly spicy special dish for her 15 dinner guests.

9. Even though she was tired, the loud buzzing noise kept her awake.

10. The Himalayas, where Mount Everest is located, are a huge, awe-inspiring mountain range in Asia.

Exercise 6.11: Comma with Quotations (page 108)

1. Yoo-Jin wrote, "These two advertisements can be compared in several aspects."
2. "The women's salaries are higher than the average salary of men in that business," asserted Nina.
3. "Excuse me," the customer asked, "where can I find the reference section?"
4. "But that was my idea!" Sachiko exclaimed.
5. "This design will appeal to young, fashionable people. We must use it in our next product," said the artist to the manager.
6. "I prefer," said Hannah, pointing at the book, "to stay at home alone to read this. It's so interesting! It's about English grammar."
7. "The style and purpose of this musical composition are fascinating," said Jessie.
8. "Online purchases were more than half of the sales in the first quarter, signifying a major new direction for the company," according to a report released by Frew and Macmillan Corporation.
9. A professor of business studies wrote, "In electronic transactions, transparency of price, design, availability, and supplier produces more choices and better pricing."
10. "Industrial development near the city is the key to our progress," announced the mayor.

Exercise 6.12: Comma with Abbreviations (page 109)

1. This course for first-year students helps with many things, e.g., study skills, time management, etc.
2. The important issue in this election is tax credits for individual citizens, i.e., indirectly returning some funds to them.
3. During the test you must remove all bags, books, papers, etc., from the desk.
4. Abbreviations should be limited to situations where they help the reader, i.e., when comprehension would be increased by using them.
5. Take some extra food, clothing, etc., on this trip because it may take longer than planned.
6. Several new books have been published recently on this topic, e.g., *The Brain's Way of Healing*.

Exercise 6.13: Comma with Contrasting or Interrupting Elements or Those Needing Separation for Clarity (page 110)

1. Amelia's husband, by contrast, is a strict vegetarian.
2. This computer, though high quality, is not the type they need.
3. Therefore, the square of the hypotenuse is equal to the sum of the squares of the other two sides.
4. Would you like to sing now, Ms. Johnson?
5. Our shoes are, you know, the best available, even if they are the most expensive.
6. Students who want to attend college must be very diligent.
7. Sounding quite excited, she spoke about her trip to New Zealand.
8. I accepted the suggestion of painting the walls red and orange because the room needed brightening.
9. Will you please be as quiet as possible during the recording?
10. Secondly, place the apples in a dish with the other fruit.
11. My flute, which I got for my 12th birthday, is one of my most prized possessions.
12. Our reading teacher bought a fine car from the second-hand car dealer on Forbes Avenue.
13. We arrived in this great city in September of 1977.
14. Angela, despite her injured foot, won the long jump.
15. This book, not the one that is on the table, is his.
16. I think that, given no serious or unexpected obstacles, we will complete our research project before the middle of March.

Exercise 6.14: Semicolon with Independent Clauses (page 111)

1. All flights in and out of the airport have been canceled; the storm is predicted to hit early this afternoon.
2. Do not go back to the beginning if you make a mistake; just keep going until you finish the job.
3. There was a variety of objects lying on the floor: old books, most of them with torn covers; sheets of paper, thrown down by the clerks; empty containers, which had obviously been used for paint; and many empty shoeboxes.
4. After the party we returned to school, driving along the old highway, a dangerous road; luckily for us, we made it back safely.
5. In order to use the machine you should first remove the dust cover; then press the green button, which starts the motor going; then turn the speed

control, at the top left, to the desired speed; and, finally, adjust the heat control to the desired temperature.

6. The traveling circus transported many things, including large tents; animals, safely secured in cages; musical instruments of all types; and costumes that were specially designed for each performer.

7. The film, which was very interesting, helped us to understand the special uses of magnetism, electricity, and heat; the presentation, as usual at such conferences, was followed by a general discussion.

Exercise 6.15: Semicolon (page 112)

1. When Stefan's order arrived, I opened the box and was surprised to find an enormous blue hiking backpack with reflective stripes; a high-tech water filtration device that included a rechargeable battery; a pair of lightweight, collapsible hiking poles; and a waterproof map of the North Country Trail.

2. A lot of money is spent on preserving our nation's water supply, which involves taking care of rivers, lakes, dams, and reservoirs; it remains a difficult task.

3. Everything went wrong yesterday: the children, who were late for school, started fighting; my car, bought just a month earlier, would not start; my best friend, recently recovered from a serious illness, called to say he was feeling sick again; and my boss, a pleasant, kind man, told me that I might lose my job.

4. The photocopier seemed to be failing: the paper kept getting jammed; there were large dark streaks in the middle of all the copies; and the machine gave an error message when it was turned on.

5. The first problem is that, in order to pay college fees, students must get loans, grants, or scholarships; and the second problem is that they must study hard to pass the difficult exams.

Exercise 6.16: Colon (page 113)

1. They purchased many things after winning the lottery: two new cars, a vacation home and a boat.

2. She read two long novels over her winter break: *Anna Karenina* and *The Tale of Genji.*

3. Our class meets on Tuesdays at 9:45, not 8:45.

4. In the introduction to his famous book, *The Origin of the Species*, Charles Darwin begins:

When on board H.M.S. "Beagle," as a naturalist, I was much struck with certain facts in the distribution of the organic beings inhabiting South America, and in the geological relations of the present to the past inhabitants of that continent. These facts, as will be seen in the latter chapters of this volume, seemed to throw some light on the origin of the species—that mystery of mysteries, as it has been called by one of our greatest philosophers.

5. The young boy had the following in his pockets: string, used chewing gum, pebbles, a catapult, some pennies, twigs, a broken pencil, and a few marbles.

6. The Japanese poet Basho once said: "Do not seek to follow in the footsteps of the wise; seek what they sought."

7. Professor Nicholas began to write the recommendation letter for her best student, which began,

    To the Admissions Committee:
    I am writing in support of Clara Morgan's application to your PhD program in Civil Engineering.

8. For this recipe, use a ratio of 3:1 (three to one)—three parts water and one part rice.

9. The odds against my horse winning are 5:2 (five to two).

10. As Ismael cleaned his room, he found the following items under the bed: a dirty sock, two of his favorite comic books, and the homework assignment he could not find the night before.

11. To his surprise, Guiseppe found three English proverbs that referred to Rome: "All roads lead to Rome," "Rome was not built in a day," and "When in Rome, do as the Romans do."

12. Leilani's daily work schedule is as follows: check for mail, reply to urgent letters, attend meetings, have a business lunch, work with the planning department, and finally, attend to mail orders.

Exercise 6.17: Double Quotation Marks (page 115)

1. My father reminded me, "Don't take Moore Street because it's under construction and the bridge is closed to traffic."

2. The contract states, "We reserve the right to void any service fee at our discretion."

3. Salma quietly suggested, "Maybe you should wait until you're feeling calmer to write that email. It's usually not a good idea to send a message while you're angry."

4. The phrase "burning the candle at both ends" means that someone is trying to do too many things and will probably run out of time and energy.

5. Tameka announced that everyone would be receiving a $500 bonus due to the success of the program. [Indirect quote—no quotation marks needed.]

6. "Please tell me more about your prior work experience," the manager requested.

7. "I don't know why the bus was so late," Fernando complained. "There was hardly any traffic so late at night."

Exercise 6.18: Using Single and Double Quotation Marks (page 116)

1. "I went to the little shop downtown to buy sandals for my vacation," Sachi explained. "I thought the clerk was very rude when she said, 'That's ridiculous. We don't carry sandals in the winter.' I'll never go back there again."

2. Johann read aloud the opening sentences of the story: "Elisa looked out the window. 'Sophia,' she whispered, 'I think someone's out there.'"

3. "I don't know why you're asking me these questions," the agent stated. "My lawyer told me not to discuss anything until she arrives."

4. "You didn't say, 'Come to my house at 7 pm,'" Jerrell argued. "You said, 'Let's meet at 7 pm.'"

5. Lucia boldly stood up and proclaimed, "The student committee has discussed this matter and is in agreement that that board decision is wrong."

6. "The latest update says, 'The authorities will provide more information when it becomes available,' but there's nothing else written," grumbled Mariam.

Exercise 6.19: Apostrophe (page 117)

1. The children's shoes were lined up neatly by the door.

2. The farmer's equipment was damaged in the flood, and he didn't know how he'd finish the harvest.

3. Aria wasn't sure if Eva's phone had been repaired.

4. The football players' uniforms were yellow with black stripes.

5. "We're going to the beach on Saturday," my mother announced. "I think we'll all benefit from getting out of the city."

6. Thomas didn't realize that his passport had expired until after he'd bought a plane ticket.

7. All of the country's leaders will gather at the Prime Minister's residence next week, where they'll discuss the many issues that the citizens are facing.

Bibliography

Beeler, C. (2017, July 21). A super-simple strategy may be key to fighting climate change. *PRI's The World*. Retrieved from www.pri.org/stories/2017-07-21/super-simple-strategy-may-be-key-fighting-climate-change

Kitchakarn, O. (2016). How students perceive social media as a learning tool in enhancing their language learning performance. *TOJET: The Turkish Online Journal of Educational Technology, 15*, 53–60. Retrieved from https://eric.ed.gov/?id=EJ1117631

Panko, B. (2017, July 20). Humans have produced nine billion tons of plastic and counting. *Smithsonian.com*. Retrieved from www.smithsonianmag.com/smart-news/humans-are-burying-earth-under-billions-tons-plastic-180964125/

Unger, E. (2017, May 3). These salt flats are one of the most remarkable vistas on earth. *National Geographic*. Retrieved from www.nationalgeographic.com/travel/destinations/south-america/bolivia/how-to-see-salar-de-uyuni-salt-flats-bolivia/